Betrayal At Bethesda

Betrayal At Bethesda

THE INTERTWINED FATES OF JAMES
FORRESTAL, JOSEPH MCCARTHY,
AND JOHN F. KENNEDY

―――

J. C. Hawkins

ISBN-13: 9781974465064
ISBN-10: 1974465063
Library of Congress Control Number: 2017912818
CreateSpace Independent Publishing Platform
North Charleston, South Carolina

For Rylan: the best buddy a man could ever ask for.

Table of Contents

Preface: A Fresh Look at American History

———

IN THE MIDDLE OF THE twentieth century, three American leaders emerged as the vanguard in the fight against global communism: James V. Forrestal, Joseph R. McCarthy, and John F. Kennedy.

These three patriots shared much in common: all were Irish-American Catholics raised in families that valued patriotism, embraced their faith, and worked hard to improve their lives.

But they differed in background and style. While Forrestal and Kennedy were Democrats, McCarthy was a Democrat-turned-Republican. Kennedy was born into a wealthy family, whereas Forrestal and McCarthy were self-made men with humble origins.

All three were military veterans. Forrestal volunteered for the US Navy in World War I and became an aviator. Yet he never served in combat, spending his time in the Office of Naval Operations in Washington, DC. That experience would serve him well in later years when he became secretary of the navy during World War II and then the nation's first secretary of defense under President Harry Truman.

On the other hand, McCarthy and Kennedy both served in the Pacific Theater during World War II, based in the Solomon Islands.

While serving as a district judge in Wisconsin, McCarthy volunteered for the US Marine Corps.

He was commissioned as a first lieutenant and trained as an intelligence officer for a dive-bomber squadron. By flying on a number of combat missions and serving at times as a tail gunner, he earned the Distinguished Flying Cross medal.

McCarthy received the following citation from Admiral Chester W. Nimitz, commander in chief of the US Pacific Fleet:

> For meritorious and efficient performance of duty as an observer and rear gunner of a dive bomber attached to a Marine scout bombing squadron operating in the Solomon Islands area from September 1 to December 31, 1943. He participated in a large number of combat missions, and in addition to his regular duties, acted as aerial photographer. He obtained excellent photographs of enemy gun positions, despite intense anti-aircraft fire, thereby gaining valuable information, which contributed materially to the success of subsequent strikes in the area. Although suffering from a severe leg injury, he refused to be hospitalized and continued to carry out his duties as Intelligence Officer in a highly efficient manner. His courageous devotion to duty was in keeping with the highest traditions of the Naval Service.

After enlisting in the US Navy, JFK achieved notoriety for his heroism as skipper of PT 109 when his vessel was cut in half by a Japanese destroyer and he led his crew to safety after abandoning the sinking boat. He earned the Navy and Marine Corps Commendation Medal that included this citation from Navy Secretary James Forrestal on May 19, 1944:

For extremely heroic conduct as Commanding Officer of Motor Torpedo Boat 109 following the collision and sinking of that vessel in the Pacific War Theater on August 1–2, 1943. Unmindful of personal danger, Lieutenant Kennedy unhesitatingly braved the difficulties and hazards of darkness to direct rescue operations, swimming many hours to secure aid and food after he had succeeded in getting his crew ashore. His outstanding courage, endurance and leadership contributed to the saving of several lives and were in keeping with the highest traditions of the United States Naval Service.

Both McCarthy and Kennedy would have to contend with war-related injuries for the rest of their lives. In both cases, these injuries may have played a role in their demise.

Forrestal and Kennedy enjoyed Ivy League educations, with both attending Princeton University. Forrestal came to Princeton after beginning his education at Dartmouth. He left Princeton just short of getting a degree. Kennedy transferred from Princeton after his freshman year to attend and graduate from Harvard. McCarthy earned his bachelor and law degrees at Marquette University while working his way through school.

Their education and military service ultimately led all three to the world of politics, where they forged a kinship in the fight against global communism. Upon the elections of Kennedy and McCarthy to the Congress in 1946, Forrestal served as a mentor to his younger colleagues. He'd already become very well acquainted with JFK on a trip to Germany in 1945 to survey war damage.

There is much more to their individual stories. But these men were clearly driven by a vision of a strong America as a global beacon of freedom in a world darkened by totalitarianism.

That vision led them all to apparent betrayal and a tragic fate at the same place: the National Naval Medical Center in Bethesda, Maryland, just outside our nation's capital. It's my intention to explore the likelihood that three of the most heinous crimes in American history may have occurred at that Bethesda hospital over a fourteen-year span.

These likely crimes are as follows:

* The May 22, 1949, death of former secretary of defense James V. Forrestal in an unexplained fall from the sixteenth floor of the tower at Bethesda, for which a naval investigative board report cited no cause. Many have speculated his death was a suicide. Others, including me, believe it was something more sinister.
* The May 2, 1957, death of US senator Joseph R. McCarthy from acute hepatitis that the hospital said was noninfectious, for which no cause was given. Media hostile to the senator insinuated the cause was alcoholism. But the death came as a huge surprise to his colleagues. No autopsy was conducted to conclusively determine the cause of the acute hepatitis. I offer compelling evidence of what was certainly foul play.
* The November 22, 1963, autopsy of assassinated president John F. Kennedy, which resulted in misleading conclusions by the Warren Commission, ignoring the eyewitness descriptions of the president's wounds by Dallas emergency room physicians, Secret Service agents, navy corpsmen who handled the body at Bethesda, FBI agents, and the embalmer at the DC mortuary.

What is especially disturbing about their deaths is the close link and friendship among all three. That friendship leads this researcher to consider there may have been nothing random about their fates. All three men inspired intense emotions, ranging from great admiration to all-consuming hatred.

This book presents a theory regarding the truth behind these events at Bethesda and how vital information related to them was hidden for more than a half century.

My theory builds on the heroic efforts of many researchers who've uncovered various elements of this troubling history. The bibliography provides a list of the books and authors examined during the course of my research.

For the first time, I provide a synthesized analysis to fill gaps that have existed for decades. Looking at these events with a critical eye led me to see the many puzzle pieces that now fit together into a new look at our Cold War history.

Critics will demand hard proof of the assertions in this book, which is not intended as a historical document. My purpose is to establish a theory I believe serious historians must scrutinize and analyze.

I offer a fair analysis of proven facts in each instance while acknowledging additional research is needed for definitive confirmation. This daunting task is simply beyond the capability of one man. I urge others to join in.

My theory will shock you. It dispels accepted beliefs in a false historical narrative long adopted as conventional wisdom. In truth, the American educational system has been the vehicle for this grand deception by brainwashing generations of young Americans about these brave leaders who led the fight against global communism and its quest for world domination.

James Forrestal carries the label of a mentally disturbed individual who killed himself. Joe McCarthy is besmirched as a witch-hunting drunkard and bully. John Kennedy endures a second assassination, this time of his character because of shortcomings in his personal life.

In many respects, history has treated them unfairly because much of our modern history has been and is being crafted by left-leaning academic ideologues with hidden agendas.

However, the true historical record eventually will come into focus. It will show all three were correct about the infiltration of the American government and leading institutions by Communists who did not have the best interests of our country at heart.

Beginning with Forrestal's death, I will explain how both McCarthy and Kennedy were heavily influenced by that event and how the demise of Joe McCarthy ultimately had a great impact on the life and fate of John Kennedy.

My hope is that readers will learn the extent of communist penetration in America was wider than has been generally acknowledged. No doubt it would have been even more malevolent if not for these three intrepid leaders and the patriotic men and women they motivated.

I pray the courage and patriotism of James V. Forrestal, Joseph R. McCarthy, and John F. Kennedy will inspire future generations of Americans as they learn truths that have been hidden or obscured for far too long.

J. C. Hawkins
St. Augustine, Florida

CHAPTER 1

Three Men—James V. Forrestal Mentors Joseph R. McCarthy and John F. Kennedy

THREE MEN BOUND BY SHARED values: Irish-American Catholicism, distinguished service in the armed forces, staunch patriotism, fervent anticommunism, and a burning love for the United States of America.

Three men bound for a similar fate and a final destination: each would die an untimely, painful death, and their dead bodies would wind up in the same location: the National Naval Medical Center in Bethesda, Maryland.

A particularly interesting tie among these three great leaders is that Forrestal served as inspiration and mentor to the younger McCarthy and Kennedy when they joined the Congress after the 1946 election.

Prior to that, Kennedy and Forrestal had forged a relationship toward the end of World War II, thanks to Forrestal's existing friendship with former Wall Street colleague Joseph P. Kennedy, Jack's father. It only deepened as Congressman Kennedy began his service to the people of his Massachusetts congressional district.

Let's briefly review how Forrestal began his cultivation of Kennedy and McCarthy as protégés.

FORRESTAL AND KENNEDY

In his pre-government days as a leading Wall Street executive, James Forrestal became well acquainted and friendly with fellow Democrat Joseph P. Kennedy.

Forrestal was president of Dillon, Read & Company, a leading international investment-banking firm. The elder Kennedy served as the first head of the Securities and Exchange Commission (SEC).

Their friendship blossomed and continued as both men furthered their careers in government service under the presidency of Franklin Delano Roosevelt (FDR). Upon the death of Navy Secretary Frank Knox, then under secretary Forrestal became secretary of the navy on May 19, 1944. Kennedy was appointed ambassador to Great Britain in 1938 and served two years before returning to private business.

Kennedy's eldest son, Joe Jr., had a distinguished career as a navy pilot that ended tragically on August 12, 1944. A bomber he piloted blew up over the English Channel before his scheduled parachuting from the plane upon launching the specially outfitted aircraft to act as a missile against the Nazi V-1 missile base in Belgium.

The death deprived the elder Kennedy of his fondest wish that young Joe would one day become president of the United States. As we would see, that mantle came to rest on his younger brother Jack.

Knowing how Joe Kennedy felt about his oldest son, Forrestal gave instructions for two priests to deliver the news of Joe Jr.'s death to the elder Kennedy at his home in Hyannis Port.

On September 5, 1944, in a private handwritten note to his good friend Jim Forrestal, Kennedy confided, "Joe's death has shocked me beyond belief...All my children are equally dear to me, but there is something about the first born that sets him a little apart—he is for always a bit of a miracle...He represents our youth, its joys and problems."

Jack had previously enlisted in the navy and ended up being commissioned as an ensign in the naval reserve. He subsequently was assigned to the Office of Naval Intelligence in Washington, DC. While living there, he got to see Secretary Forrestal on several social occasions.

Upon Jack's return from the US Navy and his recuperation from the injuries related to his extraordinary heroism in saving the crew of PT 109, Joe Kennedy arranged for Forrestal to meet with Jack in Paris and for Jack to accompany Forrestal on a trip to Germany.

Young Kennedy had signed on with the Hearst news organization as a reporter. Forrestal was headed to Germany for the Potsdam Conference of the Allies and a tour of the war-damaged country.

During the flight from Paris to Berlin, Forrestal asked Kennedy about his view of Clement Atlee, who would oust Winston Churchill as prime minister in the British election. Forrestal found JFK's insights very impressive.

The trip proved formative in molding Jack Kennedy into a staunch anticommunist. With the keen eye of the journalist he'd become, he recorded his observations in a diary that did not become public until 1995.

Upon arrival in Berlin on July 28, 1945, Jack was moved by the utter devastation in the German capital and the plight of the local population trying to survive on meager food rations.

Kennedy was particularly appalled at the behavior of the Soviets in their occupation: "The Russians moved in with such violence at the beginning—stripping factories and raping women—that they alienated the German members of the Communistic Party, which had some strength in the factories."

As had been feared earlier by General George S. Patton Jr. (who opposed FDR's policies regarding the German occupation), Kennedy noted the atrocities that took place: "The Russians have pretty well plundered the country, have been living off it…The Russians have been taking all the able-bodied men and women and shipping them away."

After the Potsdam Conference ended, Forrestal and Kennedy made their way to Bremen, a major German port and industrial center. There he reported that the Russians were not the only occupation forces carrying out looting: "The British had gone into Bremen ahead of us—and everyone was unanimous in their description of British looting and destruction, which had been very heavy."

JFK was equally distressed to learn American troops had participated in the looting as well.

After touring Bremen and Bremerhaven, Forrestal and Kennedy flew to Bavaria to visit the town of Berchtesgaden and then drove to see Hitler's mountain retreat, Eagle's Nest.

One highlight of the trip was the opportunity to accompany Forrestal to an August 1 meeting with Supreme Allied Commander Dwight Eisenhower. No one could imagine at the time this first real meeting of two future presidents of the United States, although they likely shook hands briefly when Eisenhower was on hand to greet Forrestal upon his arrival in Germany.

Kennedy recorded the following remarkable item in his diary on August 1, 1945:

After visiting these places, you can easily understand how that within a few years Hitler will emerge from the hatred that surrounds him now as one of the most significant figures who ever lived. He had boundless ambition for his country, which rendered him a menace to the peace of the world but he had a mystery about him in the way that he lived and in the manner of his death that will live and grow after him. He had in him the stuff of which legends are made.

It was clear that young Kennedy had been influenced by his father's views regarding the Nazi dictator and the course of events leading up to World War II.

The Kennedy diary holds yet another surprise. In an entry titled "Impressions of Berlin Ruins," JFK made the following astonishing disclosure:

Hitler's Reich Chancellery was a shell. The walls were chipped and scarred by bullets, showing the terrific fight that took place at the time of its fall. Hitler's air raid shelter was about 120 feet down in the ground—well furnished but completely devastated. The room where Hitler was supposed to have met his death showed scorched walls and traces of fire. There is no complete evidence, however, that the body that was found was Hitler's body. The Russians doubt that he is dead.

Upon the Forrestal party's return to London, JFK fell ill with a high malarial fever at the Grosvenor House Hotel. Forrestal was greatly concerned and stayed with young Kennedy until he could recover enough to fly back to the States in Forrestal's plane on August 6.

In appreciation, JFK wrote the following note to Secretary Forrestal:

Dear Mr. Secretary,

I am sorry that I did not get the opportunity at the airport to say goodbye—and thank you.

I appreciate more than I can [say] your taking me—and your consideration on the trip itself.

It was a great opportunity, and I'll always remember it as about as interesting a two weeks as I have ever had. Again my thanks,

Sincerely, Jack Kennedy

On December 27, 1945, Joe Kennedy and Forrestal met for a round of golf in Palm Beach. Forrestal recorded in his diary that Kennedy believed there would have been no war in Western Europe had FDR and Winston Churchill not forced British Prime Minister Neville Chamberlain to face down the Germans over Poland.

Kennedy made clear his belief that if left to his own devices, Hitler would have turned his attention to the East toward the Soviet Union instead of going to war with Britain.

With his firsthand look at the Soviet savagery in Germany, as well as discussions with Forrestal regarding the future threats posed by a victorious Soviet Union, Jack Kennedy was on his way to a political career that he'd launch as "the Fighting Conservative."

At the official end to World War II, after the fall of Japan, Jack sent Forrestal a congratulatory note with a box of cigars.

Forrestal replied on September 8, 1945, with a letter asking the following: "What are your plans? Do you want to do any work here—if so why don't you come down and see what there is on hand? Regards to your father."

Kennedy didn't follow up on the prospective offer of a job with the Navy Department. Instead, he set his sights on politics.

Nonetheless, the relationship between Forrestal and the younger Kennedy continued to grow.

Jack Kennedy won election to the US House of Representatives from the Eleventh District in Massachusetts by handily defeating Republican Lester Bowen, with a vote total of 69,093 to 26,007. Forrestal sent a congratulatory telegram to the new congressman, saying, "Dear Jack, Congratulations. I am delighted that you survived."

Just after Jack's election to Congress, he was house hunting in Washington, DC, when it was time to return to Hyannis Port for Thanksgiving. Faced with overbooked planes, Jack called Forrestal to see if he might get a ride on Forrestal's plane to New England.

Young Kennedy met the Forrestals at Anacostia Naval Air Station and flew with them to Newport, Rhode Island. From there, Kennedy motored on to Hyannis Port.

According to James Kelley, a JFK campaign aide who accompanied them on the ride, the conversation on the plane centered on the menace posed by global communism.

As Congressman-elect Kennedy, Jack was outspoken. He vowed on many occasions that America could never submit to a "small clique of ruthless, powerful and selfish men" running "a slave state." The "Fighting Conservative" was ready for the challenges ahead.

His words were eerily prophetic about behind-the-scenes cabals, what today many call "the Deep State."

Forrestal and McCarthy

After the election of 1946, two young World War II veterans headed to Washington, DC, to take their places in the US Congress. Jack Kennedy and Joe McCarthy were coming to the nation's capital to make a lasting impression on the country.

Joe McCarthy was the new US senator from Wisconsin, having beaten incumbent Republican Robert La Follette Jr., in the GOP primary and, then, Democrat Howard J. McMurray in a landslide in the general election.

Upon arrival in Washington two weeks prior to being sworn in as a senator, McCarthy was surprised to receive a luncheon invitation from Navy Secretary Forrestal.

Looking back on that meeting, McCarthy mused, "I have often wondered how the extremely busy Secretary of the Navy discovered that a freshman Senator had arrived in town and why he took so much time out to discuss the problems which were so deeply disturbing him. More than an equal number of times I have thanked God that he did."

He continued, "Before meeting Jim Forrestal I thought we were losing to international Communism because of incompetence and stupidity on the part of our planners. I mentioned that to Forrestal. I shall forever remember his answer. He said, 'McCarthy, consistency has never been a mark of stupidity. If they were merely stupid they would occasionally make a mistake in our favor.' This phrase struck me so forcefully that I have often used it since."

During their discussions, Forrestal made it clear that he did not approve of FDR's capitulation at Yalta and that other key American leaders were ceding too much to Soviet dictator Stalin.

In his landmark book *The Assassination of Joe McCarthy*, author Medford Evans recounted that Forrestal named individuals he considered known Communists in key government leadership positions. They included Treasury official Harry Dexter White and White House aide Lauchlin Currie.

In his book *America's Retreat from Victory*, McCarthy documented a strong attack on General George C. Marshall as a key figure in advancing procommunist policies in the State Department. In response to an inquiry regarding what Forrestal had told him about

Marshall, McCarthy said, "Forrestal told me he was convinced that General Marshall was one of the key figures in the United States in advancing Communist objectives."

McCarthy asserted in his book that the Roosevelt administration, including General Marshall, had advance warning of the pending Japanese attack on Pearl Harbor as early as December 4. For unknown reasons, President Roosevelt and Marshall did not pass the information along to Admiral Husband E. Kimmel and General Walter Short, the US commanders in Hawaii.

No doubt James Forrestal was aware of this deceit as well.

CHAPTER 2

Why Did a Great Patriot, James Forrestal, Have to Die So Tragically?

———

IN THE AFTERMATH OF WORLD War II, being both an ardent anticommunist and outspoken critic of US foreign policy came with a high price: risk of death.

There is no greater example of this sad fact than the apparent brutal murder of former defense secretary James V. Forrestal and its subsequent cover-up.

Early in the morning of May 22, 1949, James Forrestal fell to his death from a sixteenth-floor window at Bethesda Naval Hospital, where he was being treated for "depression."

The almost immediate reaction in the media was to portray the death as suicide by a highly troubled man. This slanderous narrative was promoted by a hostile leftist press led by smear master Drew Pearson, who had hounded Forrestal mercilessly for years. (Pearson would direct his scurrilous lying against Joe McCarthy and Jack Kennedy as well over the coming years.)

An official US Navy medical review board concluded it could not establish a cause for the fall. The autopsy report was not made public. The complete report of the board, known as the Willcutts Report, was withheld from public release until 2004.

Subsequent independent research by several investigators, led by Washington economist and political commentator David Martin, reveals the suicide theory simply doesn't hold up under scrutiny.

Inexplicably, Forrestal's body was found with the belt from his bathrobe wrapped around his neck. He had fallen approximately thirteen stories to land on what was alternately described as the roof of part of the building or a ledge.

Among the lingering questions are:

* Why was no special security assigned for a former high-government official, a man allegedly suffering from severe depression?
* Why was Forrestal placed in the VIP suite on the sixteenth floor of the hospital if he was potentially suicidal?
* Why on the night of his death did hospital apprentice R. W. Harrison, a new attendant on the third shift watch, leave his post during the time that Forrestal died?

The naval review board conducted no investigation into the backgrounds of those who were in the hospital that evening. There was no attempt to determine if Forrestal's death might have been the result of a criminal act. Its bias was clearly toward suicide.

None of the other patients on the sixteenth floor were interviewed to determine if they had heard or seen anything out of the ordinary.

There are discrepancies around the assertion by some media that Forrestal had been hand copying a poem he'd been reading that evening. A subsequent review by Martin of the handwriting of the alleged transcribed poem and available samples of Forrestal's writing suggests the handwritten poem copy was a forgery.

One naval corpsman said that when he looked in on Forrestal, the patient was asleep in bed, an observation at variance with false media reports of Forrestal copying the poem.

George Raines, the attending psychiatrist, helped push the poem-copying narrative. His overall characterization of Forrestal's condition is highly suspect. He was not at the hospital at the time of Forrestal's death.

Raines prescribed a regimen for Forrestal that didn't seem to work all that well:

Week one: narcosis with sodium amytal.

Weeks two through five: a regimen of insulin subshock with psychotherapeutic interviews.

Week four: insulin administered only in stimulating doses; ten units of insulin four times a day, morning, noon, afternoon, and evening.

Raines reported that Forrestal overreacted to the insulin and the amytal, which would occasionally throw him into a confused state with a great deal of agitation.

The doctor noted that he considered electroshock treatment but decided to postpone it for another ninety days out of concern that Forrestal might become even more depressed and suicidal.

While staff members reported Forrestal's mood improving and noted a weight gain, one has to wonder exactly why Raines pursued the course he did.

Narcosis with sodium amytal essentially means sedating the patient into a state of drowsiness or unconsciousness. Sodium amytal is now known as amobarbital, a barbiturate derivative with sedative-hypnotic properties.

Interestingly enough, when given intravenously, sodium amytal is what's called "the truth serum." So, in week one, were Raines and others trying to get information from Forrestal without his knowledge or permission?

Back in the 1940s and 1950s, psychiatrists used insulin subshock as a means of sedating patients before psychotherapy. In general, the dosage was just enough to control the patient without having him go into a coma.

Pumping a patient full of insulin over several weeks also would result in the patient gaining weight.

It's likely Raines didn't reveal the reason for keeping personal visitors like a Catholic priest away from Forrestal. Probably he didn't want people on the outside to conclude Forrestal was essentially a drugged prisoner, not a patient.

Nurse Dorothy Turner testified she'd seen broken glass on the bed on the night of Forrestal's death, perhaps suggestive of a struggle occurring in the room. But almost immediately after Forrestal's body was found, his room was cleaned and the bed stripped of its linens, and no effort was made to secure the room, which may have been a potential crime scene.

Ms. Turner also noted that Forrestal seemed cheerful and in good spirits the night before his death, which is indicative of him no doubt looking forward to his discharge from the hospital and leaving with his brother Henry for some rest in the countryside.

It would surprise no neutral observer that something criminal and very dark occurred on May 22, 1949. Forrestal had made serious and dangerous enemies during his tenure in Washington.

As secretary of the navy under President Roosevelt, Forrestal saw up close and firsthand how American policy was tilted toward furthering the ambitions of Soviet dictator Joseph Stalin and frustrating the aims of our key ally, Winston Churchill of Great Britain.

He also was horrified by Roosevelt's plans to destroy Germany's capacity to rebuild its industrial economy and turn the country into an agrarian state. Treasury Secretary Henry Morgenthau put forth the Morgenthau Plan in the fall of 1944 calling for the partition of Germany into four sectors run by the United States, the Soviet Union, France, and Great Britain, along with the dismantling of Germany's industrial capacity, which would result in the displacement of hundreds of thousands of workers and their families.

A key proponent of the Morgenthau plan was Deputy Treasury Secretary Harry Dexter White, whose treasonous actions on behalf of the Soviet Union would ultimately be uncovered after the war.

Forrestal saw the plan as inhumane, unworthy of a great nation like America. In his eyes, it provided an incentive for the Germans to fight to the very last man, thus prolonging the war and increasing the loss of American soldiers' lives.

This view was shared by General George S. Patton, whose outspokenness regarding the Morgenthau Plan and the Soviet Army's entry into Berlin angered both FDR and Supreme Allied Commander Dwight D. Eisenhower. *Interestingly enough, Patton met his own untimely demise under suspicious circumstances.*

Roosevelt and Morgenthau were eager for revenge, as well as wanting to please Stalin. Writing to Queen Wilhelmina of the Netherlands on August 26, 1944, Roosevelt noted, "There are two schools of thought, those who would be altruistic in regard to the Germans, hoping by loving kindness to make them Christians again—and those who would adopt a much 'tougher' attitude. Most decidedly I belong to the latter school, for though I am not bloodthirsty, I want the Germans to know that this time at least they have definitely lost the war."

In saying he was not "bloodthirsty," Roosevelt protested too much. He apparently overlooked the devastating and inhumane aerial fire bombings of Dresden, Hamburg, and sixty-four other German cities, which resulted in an appalling loss of civilian lives. Had America lost the war, Roosevelt, Winston Churchill, and Harry Truman all could have been prosecuted as war criminals for these atrocities.

Forrestal worked behind the scenes with Under Secretary of State Joseph Grew to bring about an earlier-negotiated end to the war with Japan, which might have precluded the use of the two atomic bombs on Hiroshima and Nagasaki. Had Grew and Forrestal succeeded, the lives of many thousands of American troops who died in such bloody battles as Okinawa and Iwo Jima might have been spared as well.

A career diplomat, Grew had tried to secure a peace with Japan prior to Pearl Harbor, but was thwarted in his efforts by Harry Dexter White and Lauchlin Currie, two key aides to FDR. White and Currie were both covert Soviet agents, as revealed in FBI intercepts.

Because Roosevelt, and then Truman, were intent on working with Stalin on a postwar New World Order, they wanted to draw the Soviet Union into declaring war on Japan prior to the war's end so Stalin could participate in the postwar spoils in the Far East.

Upon the death of President Roosevelt in April 1945, Truman inherited much of the foreign policy team advising FDR, including a State Department riddled with Communists and Soviet sympathizers (see appendix A).

After the German surrender on May 8, 1945, President Truman met at Potsdam outside of Berlin with Stalin and British Prime

Minister Winston Churchill. The conference began on July 17. On July 28, Churchill was replaced by newly elected prime minister Clement Atlee. The conference ended on August 2, 1945.

As noted in chapter 1, Forrestal was not included as part of the official American delegation. So he attended on his own. He used the opportunity to visit Berlin to see the extent of war damage. He also visited Bremen, Frankfurt, Salzburg, and Hitler's mountain retreat at Berchtesgaden.

Joining him on the trip was the twenty-eight-year-old son of a good friend from his days on Wall Street—navy veteran John F. Kennedy, who was covering the Potsdam conference as a journalist for the Hearst news organization. (More detail on this trip is found in chapter 1.)

The elder Kennedy told Forrestal during a golf outing on December 27, 1945, that British Prime Minister Neville Chamberlain had told him in 1938 that England was in no position to risk going to war with Hitler.

Kennedy believed Hitler was more likely to face off against the Soviet Union instead. But William Bullitt, US ambassador to France, kept advising President Roosevelt that the Germans had to be faced down because of the invasion of Poland in 1939. Bullitt had been the first ambassador to the Soviet Union from 1933 to 1936. He was strongly pro-Soviet.

Forrestal also saw the folly of Truman's policy toward China, which resulted in the ultimate abandonment of longtime ally Chiang Kai-shek (a leader in the fight against Imperial Japan) in favor of the Communists led by Mao Tse-tung.

The Truman policy was heavily influenced by communists and their dupes in the State Department, news media, and academia.

On January 30, 1949, Democrat congressman John F. Kennedy delivered a stinging and forceful rebuke to the Truman and Roosevelt administrations' disastrous China policy that resulted in a key ally becoming a communist state, ruled by a ruthless, bloodthirsty dictator.

Clearly Kennedy's discussions with Forrestal made a lasting impression. Forrestal must have been extremely proud of his protégé.

Renowned for his excellent managerial skills and financial acumen, Forrestal was named the first secretary of defense on September 17, 1947, after the armed services were combined into a single government department.

Forrestal found himself presiding over the demilitarization effort to scale back the armed forces after the end of World War II. Alarmed by the threat posed by the Soviet Union, he was reluctant to make cuts as drastic as those advocated by President Truman.

He also locked horns with Truman and other administration officials over the creation of a separate Jewish state in the Middle East. Forrestal was concerned the creation of Israel might create difficulties in dealing with the oil-producing Arab states in the region. He knew how vital a stable oil supply was to military readiness, especially for the US Navy to maintain a global presence.

Forrestal aggressively advocated for the racial integration of the armed services, as he'd successfully done as secretary of the navy in 1944. He gained a great victory in 1948 with President Truman's executive order calling for an end to racial discrimination in the military.

His forceful style in advancing his anticommunist beliefs, his opposition to an Israeli state, and his advocacy of the need for military strength won him numerous enemies, both in government and in the left-leaning news media. National columnists Drew Pearson and Walter Winchell both undertook extensive smear campaigns against the secretary.

The many clashes took their toll. Finally, on March 28, 1949, Forrestal resigned from the Defense Department. He was emotionally and physically exhausted. Shortly afterward, he flew to Hobe Sound, Florida, to the home of Robert Lovett, where his wife was already visiting.

Lovett was a wealthy investment banker who'd become a friend during Forrestal's days on Wall Street, and then later in government service. Lovett briefly served as under secretary of state to George Marshall.

Concerned over his condition, Forrestal met with Dr. William Menninger of the Menninger Foundation and Captain George N. Raines, chief psychiatrist at the US Naval Medical Center at Bethesda.

Exhausted and emotionally spent, Forrestal was persuaded to travel to Bethesda Naval Hospital for psychiatric treatment by Dr. Raines. Raines would later confide to Dr. Robert P. Nenno, an assistant, that he had been instructed by "the people downtown" to put Forrestal in the VIP suite on the sixteenth floor of the hospital.

The unnamed "people downtown" clearly wanted to put Forrestal into virtual imprisonment, a situation from which he would not leave alive. Forrestal's brother Henry revealed in an interview with Cornell Simpson, *nom de plume* of the author of *The Death of James Forrestal,* that he was unable to visit his brother regularly, as were three of James's closest personal friends and a priest, Monsignor Maurice S. Sheehy (prelate at Catholic University in Washington).

Sheehy tried six different times to visit Forrestal at Bethesda and was never permitted to do so. However, he was able to send and receive letters from Forrestal.

Monsignor Sheehy noted the following about Forrestal: "Many, many times in his letters to me, Jim Forrestal wrote anxiously and fearfully and bitterly of the enormous harm that had been [done], and was unceasingly being done, by men in high office in the United States government, who he was convinced were Communists or under the influence of Communists, and who he said were shaping the policies of the United States government to aid Soviet Russia and harm the United States."

Clearly, hospital staff was instructed to limit Forrestal's visitors to a very limited, approved list. One visitor, whom Forrestal did not particularly like, was Texas congressman Lyndon B. Johnson. (The earlier discussion in this chapter of the treatment regimen may reveal why visitors were so restricted.)

Sheehy hurried to the hospital upon learning of Forrestal's death and relates that an unidentified navy corpsman came up to him and said, "Monsignor, you know Mr. Forrestal did not kill himself," but he quickly hurried away into the crowd of gathered people before Sheehy could engage him and learn more.

During his stay at Bethesda, Forrestal showed some improvement in his health, as evidenced by the twelve pounds he gained. He also experienced improvement in his mood. However, the weight gain may have resulted from being pumped full of insulin.

Given his progress, it was agreed that on May 22 he could leave with his brother Henry to go to a country setting to continue to regain his health.

It is the author's belief that as Henry was en route to Washington to get his brother, James Forrestal was brutally murdered, dying on the day of his scheduled discharge from the hospital and near total imprisonment.

There can be no doubt that James Forrestal, one of America's greatest patriots, died at the hands of subversive and treasonous elements within the US government.

The fact that his bathrobe belt was tied around his neck, along with the broken glass in his room that could have occurred in a struggle, is suggestive that Forrestal was roused from a sound sleep, strangled with the belt, and then thrown out the kitchen window. He was likely already dead before he was pushed out the window. None of the staff reported hearing any scream from Forrestal.

JAMES FORRESTAL MADE HIMSELF A MARKED MAN BY THE FACT THAT HE

1. believed the Japanese attack on Pearl Harbor could have been avoided and prevented. He likely was aware the highest levels of the FDR administration, including FDR, knew the Japanese were headed to Pearl Harbor and that the fleet there could have been moved in time to avoid the devastation caused by the attack;

2. opposed the Morgenthau Plan to destroy Germany forever, which was strongly supported by Supreme Allied Commander Dwight Eisenhower;

3. was aware of confirmed Communist traitors in the US government after learning of the FBI Venona intercepts of Soviet coded transmissions;

4. questioned the need for the Soviet Union to enter the war against Japan, fearing the loss of more territory and strategic advantage to Stalin;

5. opposed use of the atomic bomb on Japan, instead favoring a naval blockade to force Japan's surrender. The navy's

top admirals, William Halsey, Chester Nimitz, and William Leahy, all publicly stated after the war ended that the A-bomb was not needed to get Japan to surrender and that its use was inhumane;

6. voiced concerns that creation of a Jewish state in the Middle East would lead to a possible disruption in the flow of oil to the West. His position leads some researchers to question if militant Zionists were behind his demise;

7. formed an alliance with FBI director J. Edgar Hoover to root out Communist infiltration into the country to carry out possible atomic, biological, and chemical attacks. As secretary of defense, he convened a top secret group called the War Council of military leaders and top scientists to assess such a risk. The War Council study led to a major FBI crackdown and arrests of top American Communist Party leaders. Close to one hundred of them were convicted for violations of the 1940 Smith Act that outlawed the Communist Party;

8. remained adamantly anticommunist while his colleagues took a more conciliatory approach to the Soviet Union. Forrestal told Joe McCarthy that George Marshall "was one of the leading figures in the United States advancing Communist objectives."

FINAL CONCLUSIONS REGARDING FORRESTAL'S DEATH

Forrestal knew that Marshall and President Roosevelt had kept the army and navy leaders at Pearl Harbor in the dark regarding a possible Japanese sneak attack. Japanese messages had been decoded in advance that confirmed Pearl Harbor as the target of the Japanese military forces underway in the Pacific Ocean.

No doubt, Forrestal was well aware that FDR had the decoded messages in his possession and had read them by 9:00 p.m. on December 6, which was more than enough time to telephone Admiral Husband E. Kimmel and General Walter Short in Hawaii to alert them.

In one of the most shameful acts of treason in American history, both Kimmel and Short were scapegoated for the attack. This treachery is revealed in great detail by John Koster in his groundbreaking book *Operation Snow: How a Soviet Mole in FDR's White House Triggered Pearl Harbor.*

The broad scope of his enemies and their access to James Forrestal while highly vulnerable at Bethesda all point to a very dark conclusion: murder in the first degree by perpetrators unknown.

CHAPTER 3

The McCarthy-Kennedy Connection

———

THE TWO FORRESTAL PROTÉGÉS BECAME fast friends upon coming to Congress in 1947. Both shared a strong anticommunist conviction, with Kennedy immediately taking on a labor union executive in his early days as a congressman, earning the respect of his colleagues, especially fellow freshman congressman Richard Nixon of California.

Both McCarthy and Kennedy zeroed in on the State Department as a haven for Communist sympathizers and dupes. Before McCarthy actively went after State Department elites, JFK became very outspoken, noting in a House speech on January 28, 1949, that "the responsibility for the failure of our foreign policy in the Far East rests squarely with the White House and Department of State."

JFK followed up his House remarks with a public speech in Salem, Massachusetts, two days later. He created a major stir, and even mild sensation, with these pointed allegations:

> Our policy in China has reaped the whirlwind. The continued insistence that aid would not be forthcoming unless a coalition government with the Communists was formed was a crippling blow to the Nationalist government. So concerned were our diplomats and their advisers, the Lattimores, and

the Fairbanks, with the imperfections of the diplomatic system in China after 20 years of war, and the tales of corruption in high place, that they lost sight of our tremendous stake in a noncommunist China.

There were those who claimed, and still claim, that Chinese Communism was not really communism at all but an advanced agrarian reform movement which did not take direction from Moscow.

This is the tragic story of China whose freedom we once fought to preserve. What our young men have saved, our diplomats and our President have frittered away.

McCarthy and Nixon clearly admired their Democrat colleague, the self-styled "Fighting Conservative," for not being hesitant to take on fellow Democrat Harry Truman in the White House. Somewhere in Washington, DC, James Forrestal had to be beaming with pride as well.

ORIGINS OF THE FRIENDSHIP

There's some indication that the McCarthy-Kennedy link might have begun well before the two men joined the Congress in 1947. Roy Cohn, McCarthy's right-hand man in his efforts to root out Communists in government, revealed a very surprising story in his book on McCarthy.

Cohn wrote that, as a marine attached to the First Marine Air Wing on New Georgia in the Solomon Islands, McCarthy joined PT boat commander Kennedy on two nighttime patrols from Villa Lavella, another one of the Solomon Islands.

At that time, then lieutenant Kennedy was in command of PT 59, a replacement boat for the destroyed PT 109. Cohn claims that on the patrols, McCarthy "got to shoot the machine guns."

His source for this story was Penn T. Kimball, another marine on New Georgia who later became a journalism professor at Columbia University. In an interview with Joan and Clay Blair for their 1976 book on JFK, *In Search of JFK*, Kimball insisted the story was true.

The Blairs tracked down Col. Glenn Todd, who was McCarthy's commanding officer on New Georgia. He couldn't verify the Kimball account, but he did acknowledge McCarthy was a good marine officer and made many combat flights that he didn't have to. Todd noted McCarthy was "far from a coward, in fact, he was a brave man."

Certainly the outgoing McCarthy, with his boldness, would be the type of man to whom JFK would be attracted as a friend.

The Blairs also interviewed Senator George Smathers of Florida, a close Kennedy friend. He confirmed that Jack Kennedy had known McCarthy "for some time."

He further shared this insight: "I don't know whether it was through the Catholic Church angle, or what it was, but I always had the feeling Jack Kennedy was very sympathetic to Joe—not what Joe was saying—but sympathetic to Joe as a person. Jack liked him personally."

JFK was not the only Kennedy who developed a close friendship with McCarthy.

Joe Kennedy took an immediate liking to Senator McCarthy, seeing in him a fellow Irish-Catholic who had rightly identified the infiltration of major institutions by domestic Communists.

As their friendship developed, McCarthy became a frequent visitor to the Kennedy compounds in Palm Beach and Hyannis Port. In fact, McCarthy at times dated two of the Kennedy sisters (Eunice and Patricia) before they moved on to their eventual husbands.

Eunice enjoyed Joe's company and had him as a frequent guest at parties she hosted in Washington. He often was accompanied by his assistant Jean Kerr, who ultimately became his wife.

McCarthy formed a particularly close relationship with Robert Kennedy, who asked Joe to be the godfather to his firstborn, Kathleen, in 1951.

The Kennedy link solidified further when McCarthy hired RFK as minority counsel to the Senate Permanent Subcommittee on Investigations in December 1952. Kennedy served only until July 1953 after having run-ins with the committee's majority counsel, Cohn.

Despite his departure from the committee, RFK maintained a strong affection for McCarthy, even after McCarthy endured his downfall and censure in the Senate.

Historian Arthur Schlesinger Jr., recounted the following incident at a 1955 dinner meeting in his 1978 book *Robert Kennedy and His Times*:

Still his Irish conception of loyalty turned him against some he felt had treated McCarthy unfairly. In January 1955, Edward R. Murrow [who had issued a famous anti-McCarthy telecast the previous year] spoke at the banquet honoring those, Kennedy among them, who had been selected by the Junior Chamber of Commerce as the Ten Outstanding Young Men of 1954. Kennedy grimly walked out.

Former South Carolina senator Fritz Hollings, another honoree, recounts RFK climbing down from the bleachers where they were sitting and saying, "I wouldn't be caught dead listening to that son of a bitch." That story is retold in a 2016 RFK biography, *Bobby Kennedy, the Making of a Liberal Icon* by Larry Tye.

JFK had been involved in a similar incident three years before RFK's display when attending the one hundredth anniversary of the Harvard Spee Club dinner. (The Spee Club is a social organization at Harvard similar to a fraternity.) Robert Armory, a Kennedy administration official and attendee at the dinner, recounted the following in an oral history at the Kennedy Library: "When a speaker had likened McCarthy to the convicted Soviet spy Alger Hiss, JFK rose to his feet and declared, 'How dare you couple the name of a great American patriot with that of a traitor!' Kennedy then turned on his heel and walked out."

No doubt the Kennedy affection for McCarthy was partly in gratitude for McCarthy's magnanimous assistance in JFK's bid for the Senate in 1952. As he faced off against incumbent Republican Henry Cabot Lodge, Kennedy had to be concerned that McCarthy, a much-sought-after speaker on behalf of GOP candidates in that election, would be pressured into supporting Lodge.

McCarthy found his strong attachment to the Kennedys and his disdain for the elitist Lodge a powerful combination in deciding to not campaign for Lodge, who would be the only Republican Senate candidate not receiving McCarthy's backing.

Conservative icon William F. Buckley Jr. was with McCarthy when the senator received a phone call from the Republican National Committee seeking his support for Lodge. McCarthy declined, hung up, and made it clear to Buckley that he greatly preferred JFK.

Another event showed the strong bond between McCarthy and the Kennedys. When he married his assistant Jean Kerr on September 29, 1953, both Jack and Bobby Kennedy were in attendance at St. Matthew's Cathedral in downtown Washington, and their sister Eunice was a bridesmaid.

Other luminaries in attendance at the ceremony were Vice President and Mrs. Richard Nixon, Senator Barry Goldwater, and boxing legend Jack Dempsey. A crowd of four thousand people massed outside the church to cheer when Mr. and Mrs. McCarthy left for their wedding reception.

No doubt these many ties played on Jack Kennedy's mind when he was faced with the dilemma of joining his Democrat Senate colleagues in the effort to censure Joe McCarthy toward the end of 1954. When the vote to condemn on two counts was taken on December 2, Kennedy was absent from the Senate due to his recuperation from serious back surgery. Though pressured by his Democrat colleagues to join them in the censure effort, Kennedy could not bring himself to turn his back on his good friend.

Kennedy would not publicly criticize McCarthy until 1956, when his national ambitions began to surface, and he recognized he would need to address the matter. At the Democrat 1956 Convention, Eleanor Roosevelt, the ultimate symbol of Democrat ultraleftism and softness on communism, publicly berated JFK and continued to state her opposition to him until she reluctantly supported JFK's White House bid in 1960.

Joe McCarthy's death in May 1957 had a particularly hard effect on Bobby Kennedy. When news of his death came, RFK was in his office in the Senate Building (he worked on a major committee as counsel). He sent the office staff home for the day, retreated to his private office, and shut the door.

In his private journal, he recorded, "It was all very difficult for me as I feel I have lost an important part of my life—even though it is in the past."

Upon learning of McCarthy's death, Joe Kennedy sent the following telegram to McCarthy's widow, Jean: "Shocked and deeply grieved to hear of Joe's passing. His indomitable courage in adhering to the cause in which he believed evoked my warm admiration. His friendship was deeply appreciated and reciprocated. Rose and I extend to you our heartfelt prayers, our deepest sympathy and our warm affection. Sincerely, Joseph Kennedy"

The Kennedys' grief was shared by many Americans. McCarthy was given a rare state funeral that included a private memorial service in the US Senate chamber, with his seat covered in flowers. At St. Matthew's Cathedral, McCarthy received the highest honor of the Roman Catholic Church, a Solemn Pontifical Requiem Mass before one hundred priests and two thousand attendees. Among them were FBI director J. Edgar Hoover and seventy US senators.

Thousands of Americans lined up to pay their final respects at the viewing at a Washington, DC funeral home from early in the morning until late at night. McCarthy's wife, Jean, received more than seventy bags of mail with wishes of condolences from around the country.

Bobby Kennedy was among the mourners in Washington who made the trip to Appleton, Wisconsin, for the final funeral and burial.

Writing further in his journal, RFK noted: "He was a very complicated character. His whole method of operation was complicated because he would get a guilty feeling and get hurt after he blasted somebody…He was sensitive and yet insensitive. He didn't anticipate the results of what he was doing. He was very thoughtful of his friends and yet he could be so cruel."

Speaking of cruel, consider the fates that befell James Forrestal, Joe McCarthy, Jack Kennedy, and Bobby Kennedy.

CHAPTER 4

McCarthy's Despair over Forrestal's Death and JFK's Continued Forrestal Connection

———

JOE MCCARTHY BEGAN HIS SENATE career highly concerned about the threat posed by global communism and the inroads it had made and was making in American institutions and government. But what really motivated him into leading the charge against Communist infiltration was the shocking death of James Forrestal.

In recounting his reaction, McCarthy asserted, "The Communists hounded Forrestal to his death. They killed him just as definitely as if they had thrown him from that sixteenth-story window in Bethesda Naval Hospital. On May 22, 1949, word flashed around the world that the smashed and broken body of Jim Forrestal was found beside Bethesda Naval Hospital. We know there was a celebration in the Communist headquarters in New York that night."

He continued:

> While I am not a sentimental man, I was touched deeply and left numb by the news of Forrestal's murder. But I was affected much more deeply when I heard of the Communist celebration when they heard of Forrestal's murder. On that night, I dedicated part of this fight to Jim Forrestal. That night I said, 'Jim Forrestal, wherever you are, I promise their

victory will turn to ashes and dust.' I hope I can keep that promise. Thus I started the public phase of my fight against Communists, knowing full well exactly how they operate.

Little did Joe McCarthy know how prophetic those words would be or the fate that awaited him at Bethesda Naval Hospital in May 1957.

The Mentor's Ongoing Inspiration

We've seen the incredible impact James Forrestal had in inspiring Joe McCarthy to aggressively take on communist sympathizers and dupes.

While he did not share McCarthy's zeal in pursuing communist infiltrators, Jack Kennedy still recognized the threat global communism posed to the United States and entire Western world.

That threat was something he'd discussed at length with his mentor Jim Forrestal.

Upon becoming president in 1961, the Kennedy link to Forrestal took on new meaning with the appointment of Forrestal's son Michael as a member of JFK's national security team. JFK and Michael had developed a friendship prior to that appointment.

As a key aide to national security advisor McGeorge Bundy, Forrestal specialized in Asian affairs. He was very much involved in the increasing American presence in Vietnam.

Interestingly enough, Forrestal noted in a memorandum dated April 26, 1962, that Kennedy charged Bundy "to seize upon any favourable moment to reduce our involvement" in Vietnam. Following the assassination of his president and good friend, Forrestal wound up leaving government service in 1965.

Bundy, of course, steered the Johnson administration in another direction in Vietnam. It's worth noting he was the brother of William Bundy, a CIA operative originally targeted by Joe McCarthy.

Each Memorial Day, presidents travel to Arlington National Cemetery to honor our armed forces by placing a wreath at the Tomb of the Unknown Soldier and making appropriate remarks in tribute to the noble sacrifice of those who died in the nation's service.

In his speech that day, President Kennedy spoke these inspiring words: "The cost of freedom is always high, but Americans have always paid it. And one path we shall never choose, and that path is surrender, or submission."

Accompanying him to Arlington that day was his two-and-a-half-year-old son, John F. Kennedy Jr. One has to wonder if seeing the military pageantry that day, John-John, as millions of Americans knew and loved him, learned the salute that would touch the world on the day of his father's funeral.

On the last Memorial Day of his life, Jack Kennedy paid a solemn visit to James Forrestal's grave in Arlington National Cemetery after the conclusion of the traditional ceremonies. (A poignant photograph of the visit is available at the Kennedy Library in Boston.)

One can only wonder what went through JFK's mind as he paid homage to a man who played such a critical role in his development as a much-beloved political leader. Clearly taking the time out of his busy schedule for that visit showed the devotion he had to his mentor.

At that moment, did he possibly ponder the fate that both James Forrestal and Joe McCarthy endured at Bethesda or have any inkling of what awaited him just six months later in Dallas?

Upon completion of Memorial Day ceremonies at Arlington National Cemetery in 1963, President John F. Kennedy visited the grave of James Forrestal, his good friend and mentor, and our country's first Secretary of Defense.

Credit: Cecil Stoughton. White House Photographs. John F. Kennedy Presidential Library and Museum, Boston.

Kennedy's public devotion to Forrestal no doubt made the people either involved in or knowledgeable about Forrestal's demise quite nervous. Coupled with JFK's open hostility toward the CIA because of the Bay of Pigs fiasco and his threat to "shatter the CIA into a thousand pieces and scatter the remnants to the wind," Kennedy clearly made enemies with key figures within the CIA who possibly had a hand in the Forrestal and McCarthy deaths.

THE HIGH PRICE TO BE PAID FOR CROSSING TREACHEROUS MEN

The Bay of Pigs debacle brought things to a head, as President Kennedy decided to fire CIA director Allen Dulles, Deputy Director Charles Cabell (a retired general), and Deputy Director of Plans Richard Bissell. Both Cabell and Bissell had been assigned direct control of the operation by Dulles while the director went to a conference in Puerto Rico.

Kennedy knew that when Dulles briefed him on the Bay of Pigs plan, which had been approved previously by President Dwight Eisenhower, Dulles blatantly lied about the probability of success for the ill-fated operation.

What has been covered up by JFK critics is that President Kennedy put in place a standing order to have anti-Castro Cuban pilots fly modified B-29 bombers from Nicaragua to deliver predawn air strikes on Castro's small air force of T-33 jets before the invasion brigade landed on the beach in Cuba.

The standing order was canceled by McGeorge Bundy in a phone call to General Cabell with the proviso to postpone the mission until the invaders established a landing strip on the beach.

We can only wonder why Bundy countermanded Kennedy's direct order. Because of this treachery, Castro's jets were able to attack the invasion forces before they could establish a beachhead.

Kennedy steadfastly refused to provide American-flown air support from the offshore carrier USS *Essex* after the brigade landed on the beach because it was never part of the operational plan. He simply didn't want to break international law and create an international incident.

Yet the CIA worked with its news media stooges to blame the invasion's gross failure on JFK's decision not to authorize American air strikes from the navy carrier.

JFK had misgivings from the outset about the proposed invasion. His instincts were proved right in the execution of the plan. History has blamed JFK for not authorizing US air cover for the invasion, but Kennedy knew the risks of direct involvement by the US military were too high and the likelihood of success was low.

Unfortunately, it appears the young president raised his own risk beyond any acceptable level, as a disgruntled faction in the CIA concocted schemes of its own for revenge.

Interestingly enough, the disgraced Cabell's brother Earle was the mayor of Dallas. He was very involved in plans for the president's visit, including the motorcade route, in the days before JFK was so brutally murdered, just over two and a half years after the fiasco at the Bay of Pigs.

CHAPTER 5

A Routine Illness Claims Joe McCarthy's Life?

───

IN 1957, SENATOR JOE MCCARTHY was trying to put his political career back together after suffering censure at the hands of his Senate peers and enduring ongoing smears from a hostile news media. Little did he realize that lingering injuries incurred in World War II would soon play a role in his death.

Consider how preposterous it is for a man to go to a hospital with a knee injury at five o'clock on a Sunday afternoon and be pronounced dead five days later from acute hepatitis.

It leads one to ask, what kind of substandard medical facility and incompetent medical staff could allow such malpractice to occur? It's what you might expect in a third world country, or even worse.

We've repeatedly been told Bethesda Naval Hospital was one of the finest medical facilities in the United States. In fact, it's been the preferred facility for such personages as several presidents of the United States, as well as other leading political and military figures.

This author endeavored through the Freedom of Information Act (FOIA) to secure official documents, medical records, and statements related to Senator McCarthy's case, but was thwarted by the inability of the US Postal Service to deliver the request. More likely, the request was denied acceptance at Bethesda.

As much as the perpetrators tried to cover up the assassination of Senator McCarthy, they left far too many tracks to ignore. Foremost among these are the official statements issued by the Bethesda National Naval Medical Center.

Even though the murderers knew they could rely on the mainstream media to report what would be spoon-fed to them, the story they concocted was just too ridiculous on its face.

By following the timeline of McCarthy's hospital admission until his death, it becomes all too evident that foul play precipitated his sudden demise.

Let's review the timeline provided by news reports and see the glaring discrepancies that have existed for nearly six decades:

Sunday, April 28: Mrs. Jean McCarthy reports that her husband went to Bethesda Naval Hospital with a knee injury at 5:00 p.m. The knee problem was related to an injury sustained during World War II. He was admitted to the neurology ward with a preliminary diagnosis of "peripheral neuritis," an inflammation of the nerves. Later that evening, he was moved to a medical ward and placed in an oxygen tent. The diagnosis was changed to "acute hepatitis."

Monday, April 29: The press is admitted to Senator McCarthy's room to photograph him, but there is no sign of the oxygen tent. The *New York Times* later reports on May 1 that the oxygen tent was removed on the evening of April 30.

Tuesday, April 30: The *Associated Press* reports that Senator McCarthy was improved but remained in serious condition with a diagnosis of acute hepatitis. A hospital spokesman is quoted as saying, "His condition is considered serious but not critical. He is slightly improved from this morning, however." The spokesman further added that McCarthy is "responding well" to treatment. No indication was given for how long the senator might remain hospitalized. The same story reports that an aide in McCarthy's office noted the senator hadn't complained of being ill during the past week.

Wednesday, May 1: The *New York Times* runs a story on page 31 with the following headline: McCARTHY IMPROVES; OUT OF OXYGEN TENT.

The story noted:

Senator Joseph R. McCarthy was reported to have spent a very comfortable day at Bethesda Naval Hospital, but he was still considered seriously ill…A hospital bulletin late in the day said the Wisconsin Republican was normal and that his condition had 'improved during the day.' The Senator's illness was diagnosed as acute hepatitis, an inflammation of the liver. Another spokesman earlier in the day, however, said the Senator has been removed from an oxygen tent last night. Mr. McCarthy was placed in the tent shortly after he was admitted on Sunday. His wife visited him in the afternoon.

Thursday, May 2: The *New York Times* reports an *Associated Press* story on page 63 with the following headline: McCARTHY UNCHANGED. The copy noted: "Senator Joseph R. McCarthy was reported tonight [Wednesday] to have spent a 'fairly comfortable day' at Bethesda Naval Hospital, but his condition remains serious."

At 6:02 p.m., Joseph R. McCarthy is pronounced dead.

Friday, May 3: In a page 1 story, the *New York Times* reported:

"Washington was shocked by the Senator's sudden death. A hospital spokesman said McCarthy 'had taken a turn for the worse between 4 p.m. and 5 p.m.' There are a number of mysterious angles about Senator McCarthy's final illness. This 'hepatitis' is an internal ailment but reports from the hospital were that he was being treated in the neurology ward." The *Times* also quoted a hospital spokesman saying, "Senator McCarthy had not had the infectious type of hepatitis, but an acute form of the disease."

The hospital tried to cover its tracks with the following official statement: "Senator Joseph R. McCarthy was admitted to the US Naval Hospital 28 April 1957 with acute hepatitis following several weeks' illness at his home. He was considered seriously ill at the time of admission, and his condition progressively failed and he expired at 18:02 2 May 1957."

The official statement contains two egregious lies:

1. Senator McCarthy was admitted to the hospital with a preliminary diagnosis of peripheral neuritis, not acute hepatitis.
2. By the accounts of his family and office staff, he had not been ill at home prior to his trip to Bethesda on April 28.

Saturday, May 4: The *New York Times* reported, "The origin of the ailment was not known and no autopsy was planned." The paper reports that a hospital spokesman said, "When Senator McCarthy was admitted to the hospital last Sunday, he was sent to a neurology ward because of a preliminary diagnosis indicated he has peripheral neuritis, an inflammation of the nerve." The spokesman further noted that McCarthy was moved to a medical ward when the diagnosis was changed to acute hepatitis.

Here's another fundamental problem with Bethesda's official story: an individual who would show up at a hospital with acute hepatitis would have the following symptoms:

❀ Jaundice (yellowing of the skin and eyes)
❀ Fever
❀ Nausea and vomiting
❀ An enlarged liver

Given the preliminary diagnosis of peripheral neuritis, it's apparent the admitting physician didn't see signs of the symptoms listed above and that Senator McCarthy was clearly experiencing pain in his knee that may well have been neuritis. As the acute hepatitis would progress, the patient could suffer delirium and convulsions and possibly slip into a coma.

Press accounts shortly after McCarthy's death attributed his death to alcoholism and cirrhosis of the liver. Among those pushing that false narrative was sworn McCarthy enemy and CIA dupe Drew Pearson (who also actively smeared James Forrestal and Jack Kennedy). In time, it became the conventional wisdom that alcoholism was the cause of Joe McCarthy's sudden death.

Again, the official documents related to the medical case demolish that contention. The death certificate lists "hepatitis, acute" as the cause of death. Acute hepatitis signifies that the illness was not infectious and, therefore, likely caused by a toxin of some sort.

This is the ultimate "smoking gun." If the hepatitis was not caused by an infection but was acute, it can only mean one thing: Joseph R. McCarthy was poisoned during his stay in the hospital.

Alcohol certainly can prove toxic to the liver. In their rush to paint McCarthy as a man who drank himself to death, the dishonest media overlooked another key part of the death certificate: after the "hepatitis, acute" listing is this information: "cause unknown."

Certainly, a hospital and medical staff as prominent as Bethesda National Naval Medical Center would have been able to determine if alcoholism or cirrhosis of the liver were involved in Joe McCarthy's death. In this case they clearly were not, or else the death certificate was fraudulent.

In his landmark book *The Assassination of Joe McCarthy*, author Medford Evans laid out the timeline and speculated that a possible toxin used in the murder could have been carbon tetrachloride, a common cleaning solvent readily available in hospitals at the time of the murder.

This author's research indicates that carbon tetrachloride is capable of poisoning the liver through skin absorption, ingestion, or inhalation of its vapor. It is a severe hepatoxin (poison that damages liver cells). Acute poisoning would most likely occur through ingestion or breathing in an atmosphere highly contaminated with the vapor.

That's why the mysterious appearance and then disappearance of the oxygen tent raises suspicion that it was the vehicle for getting Senator McCarthy to breathe in a fatally toxic volume of carbon tetrachloride vapor.

Given the senator's admission to the hospital at 5:00 p.m. on Sunday and then being placed in an oxygen tent later that night, he had ample time to breathe in enough of the poison until the tent's removal on Tuesday night.

Jean McCarthy still had the responsibility of caring for their newly adopted infant daughter. So, it's likely she couldn't stay with the senator for lengthy periods during his hospitalization.

Now, one would have to assume that a treasonous individual on the hospital staff immediately alerted the perpetrators that McCarthy had been admitted to the hospital and was in a highly vulnerable position.

Given the earlier murder of James Forrestal in 1949 and the later falsification of President John F. Kennedy's autopsy at the facility, it seems clear the hospital had long been infiltrated by US intelligence agents and comrades with hidden agendas, no doubt working on behalf of what we now call the Deep State.

CHAPTER 6

Was Joe McCarthy Assassinated?
By Whom, and Why?

———

WITH THE PREPONDERANCE OF FACTS pointing to foul play in the death of Joe McCarthy, our attention turns to determining why this happened and who the likely culprits were.

Over his career, Joe McCarthy developed a long list of enemies who wished him ill. He provoked in them a great sense of fear that his anticommunist campaign was resonating strongly with the American public.

There's no question the American government, as well as major cultural and educational institutions, was riddled with Communists and dupes who did their bidding. (See appendix A.)

The release of the Venona transcripts of intercepted, decoded Soviet spy cables by the FBI reveals the depth of this treachery, which McCarthy had only begun to root out. Fearing for their livelihoods, major media figures and politicians recognized McCarthy had to be stopped in his tracks and rendered incapable of pursuing them further. They clearly didn't want him to switch his focus solely from government to also include cultural institutions.

On September 23, 1950, McCarthy said the following regarding the impact of the Yalta Conference of 1945: "Here was signed the death warrant of the young men who were dying today in the hills and valleys of Korea. Here was signed the death warrant of the young men who will die tomorrow in the jungles of Indochina."

Already McCarthy could sense the treachery that would lead to the needless deaths of young Americans in Vietnam. He had vision that many of his contemporaries lacked.

McCarthy made his greatest impact and most intense enemies when he took on former secretary of state and then secretary of defense George Marshall in a blistering speech on the floor of the US Senate on June 14, 1951.

> How can we account for our present situation unless we believe that men in high government are concerting to deliver us to disaster? This must be the product of a great conspiracy, a conspiracy on a scale so immense as to dwarf any previous such venture in the history of man. A conspiracy of infamy so black, that when it is finally exposed, its principals shall be forever deserving of the maledictions of all honest men.

He then zeroed in on Marshall as the lead culprit: "What can be made of the unbroken series of decisions and actions contributing to the strategy of defeat? They cannot be attributed to incompetence. If Marshall were merely stupid, the laws of probability would dictate that part of his decisions would serve the country's interests."

Those last words echoed the wisdom provided to McCarthy by his mentor, James Forrestal (detailed in chapter 1), describing their luncheon meeting shortly after McCarthy arrived in Washington in 1946 to take office.

The uproar caused by the speech on both sides of the political aisle carried on after McCarthy published a follow-up book for which the speech served as the foundation: *America's Retreat from Victory: The Story of George Catlett Marshall.*

Leading the charge behind the scenes against McCarthy was none other than President Dwight David Eisenhower, whose antipathy for McCarthy and his anticommunist crusade became well known not long after Ike took office in 1953.

During his campaign for the presidency in 1952, Eisenhower made a campaign appearance with McCarthy in Milwaukee on October 2, but deleted a portion of his speech in which he intended to defend his army mentor and colleague, George Marshall.

Wisconsin politicians convinced Ike to delete the Marshall reference in order to not offend McCarthy supporters. Ike reluctantly did so but always regretted it afterward.

McCarthy further earned Eisenhower's enmity by opposing three of his appointees after Ike became president. He voted against Walter Bedell Smith for under secretary of state, Harvard president James Conant for high commissioner for Germany, and Chester "Chip" Bohlen for ambassador to the USSR. All three were confirmed anyway.

As the Korean War wound down, a number of CIA personnel quit the agency in disgust over its failure to effectively confront communism and Red China. According to the recollections of McCarthy chief counsel Roy Cohn, these informants provided McCarthy with allegations the CIA had inadvertently hired a significant number of Communist double agents whose mission was to provide the agency with inaccurate information.

It appears the CIA had been duped by Soviet and Chinese intelligence operatives throughout Europe and Asia. CIA director Allen Dulles knew this information could be dynamite in McCarthy's hands.

The senator confronted Dulles in private, telling him "that CIA was neither sacrosanct nor immune from investigation." McCarthy tried to subpoena William Bundy of the CIA, who had contributed $400 to the defense fund of Alger Hiss, the notorious Communist spy in the State Department.

Bundy was the son-in-law of former secretary of state Dean Acheson. McCarthy had strongly criticized Acheson for his role in formulating the China policy that allowed the Communists to gain control, as well as his staunch defense of Soviet spy Alger Hiss. Dulles fought off the Bundy subpoena and moved behind the scenes to thwart McCarthy's attempt to uncover subversion at the agency.

A covert campaign against McCarthy was outlined in secret testimony before McCarthy's Senate committee, with minority counsel Robert F. Kennedy in charge of the hearing. Dulles's subterfuge ultimately was revealed in a declassified CIA history in 2004.

The CIA went so far as to penetrate the senator's office with a bugging device as well as a spy. The intent was to gather any dirt possible to discredit McCarthy. Dulles also told James Angleton, his head of counterintelligence, to feed disinformation to McCarthy as a means of discrediting him.

Angleton assigned James McCargar the task of planting phony reports with a CIA contractor as a means of further undermining the investigation by McCarthy. The contractor, Col. John Grombach, had been tasked by the War Department early in World War II to create a secret intelligence operation that could ultimately become a permanent spy service. The Special Service Branch then morphed finally into the Coverage and Indoctrination Branch that was better known as "the Pond."

The Pond relied on intelligence gathered from international companies, religious organizations, and societies, as well as business and professional men who wanted to help the United States. These sources didn't want to work with the Office of Strategic Services (OSS), which they felt was infiltrated by communists and Russians.

After the war and the creation of the CIA, the Pond lost its contracts with the government. Grombach had begun early in the 1950s to furnish McCarthy with the names of known security risks in the US government. That's why the CIA decided to provide phony information to discredit him and McCarthy.

Eisenhower and establishment Republicans, including Henry Cabot Lodge and Republican chairman Leonard Hall, knew they had to surreptitiously plot the downfall of Joe McCarthy, given his immense popularity with the public.

That's when Lodge arranged a meeting with Vice President Richard Nixon, White House chief of staff Sherman Adams, Attorney General Hebert Brownell, and US Army counsel John Adams on January 21, 1954, in the attorney general's office to get the plan in motion as McCarthy geared up an investigation into Communists in the US Army.

Lodge certainly had a motive for revenge because McCarthy had refused to campaign for him in the 1952 Massachusetts election for US Senate. By withholding his support, McCarthy gave a strong boost to the successful candidacy of his good friend, Jack Kennedy.

Enraged by the senator's investigation into Communist infiltration in the US Army, Eisenhower is believed to have ordered the destruction of files at Fort Monmouth that would have proven McCarthy right.

A recent biography, *Richard Nixon: The Life* by John A. Farrell, reveals the depth of Eisenhower's hatred for McCarthy through the observations of two of the men closest to Ike in the White House.

Eisenhower's brother Milton, a key adviser, once noted, "He [Ike] loathed McCarthy as much as any human being could possibly loathe another."

White House chief of staff Sherman Adams observed that the president "had an almost obsession-hatred for the reputation-smearing, raking over of the Truman and Roosevelt administrations for the mistakes and scandals of the past."

On July 30, 1954, Republican senator Ralph Flanders of Vermont introduced a resolution condemning McCarthy for "conduct unbecoming a member." His speech was provided by the National Committee for an Effective Congress, a political action committee founded in 1948 by Eleanor Roosevelt and like-minded radical leftists.

With his humiliating censure by the US Senate and the constant pounding by left-wingers in the media, Joe McCarthy was down but not out in terms of being a threat to the global communist conspiracy.

Prominent former American Communist Louis Budenz said, "The destruction of Joe McCarthy leaves the way open to intimidate any person of consequence who moves against the Conspiracy. The Communists made him their chief target because they wanted him a symbol to remind political leaders in America not to harm the Conspiracy or its world conquest designs."

Benjamin Fischer, the former chief historian at the CIA, wrote in 2015 that during the Cold War era the agency recruited hundreds of double agents from the Soviet Union, East Germany, and Cuba, who provided false intelligence that was passed on to senior policymakers.

In an article in the *International Journal of Intelligence and Counterintelligence*, Fischer noted, "The result was a massive but largely ignored intelligence failure."

Clearly, McCarthy's instincts about the CIA were correct. Despite his setbacks, he still had the desire to root out traitors at the agency.

"Tailgunner Joe" had another matter on his list to investigate: the highly suspicious death of General George S. Patton. According to well-known conservative writer Ralph De Toledano, Senator McCarthy confided to him that he was investigating what he termed as the "murder" of General Patton.

De Toledano noted that McCarthy thought the OSS (the CIA forerunner) and its British counterpart, MI-6, were involved in the plot, and that General George Marshall was well aware of it.

This revelation came in a letter from De Toledano to author Robert Wilcox while that writer was researching his book *Target Patton: The Plot to Assassinate General George S. Patton.* (Wilcox didn't include the material in his book when published in 2008. But he later added it in a postscript included in the paperback edition in 2010.)

Nothing came of the effort because McCarthy then got heavily involved in the army hearings that laid the groundwork for his downfall. But it remained an item on his list as he considered how to revive his political career.

McCarthy also set his sights on other possible threats to national security. In a speech on February 9, 1957, to the Lincoln Day dinner in Milwaukee, he detailed "a threat of enormous proportions to the safety and independence of the United States."

The senator was referring to potential ratification of American involvement in an International Atomic Energy Agency (IAEA). The concept of sharing nuclear materials was the brainchild of nuclear scientist J. Robert Oppenheimer, later revealed to be a Communist agent.

Oppenheimer was seeking an international pool of special nuclear materials to be used to promote development of nuclear energy around the world in a working partnership between the United States and the Soviet Union. President Eisenhower termed it an "Atoms for Peace" program, which became one of his pet projects. It was established July 29, 1957, ironically not long after the death of Joe McCarthy.

The IAEA now reports to the United Nations General Assembly and Security Council, with the understanding it will inhibit proliferation of nuclear weaponry. In recent times we've witnessed how inept it's been with regard to North Korea and Iran.

As long as he was drawing a breath, Joe McCarthy was detested by the global Communist conspiracy and was the target of its sympathizers and agents in the United States. When the opportunity to eliminate him once and for all presented itself at Bethesda Naval Hospital, the culprits sprang into action with the obvious aid of hospital insiders.

Still the object of derision and scorn today because of leftist indoctrination in our school systems and continuous smears by the news media and Hollywood, Joseph McCarthy has been vindicated by facts and the truth as having been an honest patriot, one honored for his military service in World War II by Admiral Chester Nimitz, commander in chief of the Pacific Fleet, for his "courageous devotion to duty...in keeping with the highest traditions of the naval service."

Media lies have tried to paint the Nimitz citation as a phony document prepared by McCarthy, just as such smear artists as Drew Pearson and Walter Winchell first besmirched James Forrestal before training their sights on "Tailgunner Joe."

Pearson was especially virulent in his pursuit of McCarthy, which led to confrontations between the two, including a fight at a charity dinner at the Sulgrave Club in December 1950. McCarthy pummeled the older, smaller Pearson with a knee to the groin and a hard slap across the face.

Intervening in the struggle was Richard Nixon, who pulled McCarthy away from Pearson. Nixon told friends he's never seen anyone slapped that hard. Allegedly, McCarthy turned to Nixon and said, "That one was for you, Dick," acknowledging that Pearson was also antagonistic toward Nixon.

Pearson sued McCarthy, which just further sharpened the feud between the two. Attacking Pearson as a smear artist, McCarthy concentrated particular attention on Pearson staff member David Karr, who would later be revealed to be a source for the KGB. McCarthy dubbed Karr as Pearson's "KGB controller."

Karr ultimately became a successful international financier, thanks to his association with billionaire oilman Armand Hammer, who ultimately was revealed as a Soviet agent.

The most effective hit piece on McCarthy was done by Edward R. Murrow of *CBS*. On his popular *See It Now* program, Murrow selectively used clips to show the senator in the worst possible light, a tactic that later became a *CBS* hallmark with its *60 Minutes* program.

The program made Murrow an even bigger hero among liberals and those inclined to look the other way when it came to the existence of Communists in the government and other leading institutions. It also set the tone for a new style of television journalism in which any pretense at objectivity went by the boards.

What most aren't aware of is Murrow's motivation to attack McCarthy so directly and viciously. As a younger man, Murrow went to work for the Institute of International Education (IIE) after being recruited by cofounder Stephen Duggan. The organization worked on student exchanges and teacher education.

In the process of working there from 1932 to 1935, Murrow became a close friend with Duggan's son Laurence. Part of Murrow's work involved summer sessions in the Soviet Union in 1934 and similar ones planned for 1935. The Duggans were key members of the Eastern Establishment and provided Murrow with entrée into his radio career.

As Laurence Duggan moved into successively more powerful positions within the State Department, he became involved in espionage for the Soviet Union. In 1944 he left the State Department for a United Nations position and soon moved to the IIE, where he succeeded his father as president.

The House Un-American Activities Committee started looking into Duggan following revelations by Whittaker Chambers and Elizabeth Bentley, both former Soviet spies who identified Alger Hiss as a traitor. On December 11, 1948, the FBI interviewed Duggan about the allegations.

With his elite world collapsing around him, Laurence Duggan allegedly leapt to his death from his sixteenth floor office in Manhattan on December 20, 1948. The New York Police Department report noted that he "accidentally fell or jumped." The ambiguity leads some to speculate that perhaps Duggan was murdered so he couldn't reveal what he knew about the extent of Soviet spying in the United States.

Murrow was devastated by the death of his good friend, becoming enraged at those looking into Communist infiltration of America with a special hatred for Joe McCarthy.

Despite the overwhelming evidence that McCarthy had raised a critical security issue for the United States, the leftists in charge of the news media, academia, and entertainment kept up their barrage against McCarthy, which further emboldened his political opposition and, ultimately, his murderers.

As George Patton and James Forrestal found out before McCarthy and John F. Kennedy would find out just a few years later, standing up to a globalist establishment and Deep State tainted by treachery carried the heaviest of prices.

CHAPTER 7

How McCarthy's Death Influenced JFK's Fate

———

In 1953, FBI DIRECTOR J. Edgar Hoover alerted Joe McCarthy some CIA officers had past associations with left-wing organizations that were concerning. The CIA's Office of Policy Coordination (OPC) run by Frank Wisner was referred to as "Wisner's gang of weirdos" by Hoover.

McCarthy began looking into Wisner's links with a Romanian princess who was an alleged Soviet agent during World War II. Not long afterward, the Wisconsin senator became suspicious of members of the CIA's Georgetown clique, soon claiming that the CIA was a "sinkhole of Communists."

President Eisenhower dispatched Vice President Richard Nixon to handle contact with McCarthy and work to dissuade him from an investigation of Communist infiltration in the CIA. What no doubt was concerning Eisenhower was the knowledge that the CIA's forerunner organization, the Office of Strategic Services (OSS), was heavily infiltrated by Communists during World War II (see appendix A).

Working with his next-door neighbor, former CIA director Walter Bedell Smith, Nixon was able to shift the focus of investigation away from the intelligence community. Smith had been chief of staff for Supreme Allied Commander Dwight Eisenhower during

World War II. He then served as US ambassador to the Soviet Union after the war before taking over as head of the CIA in 1950 and serving until February 1953, when he was succeeded by Allen Dulles.

The ultimate irony here is that among McCarthy's list of targets were individuals who've since been linked by some researchers to the assassination of President John F. Kennedy, a dear friend of Joe McCarthy and a staunch anticommunist as well.

McCarthy made his first move against the CIA in July 1953 when he focused on William Bundy as a potential security risk. Bundy's contribution to an Alger Hiss defense fund raised McCarthy's suspicions. But he erred in selecting a member of the inner circle of Ivy League-educated CIA analysts favored by CIA director Allen Dulles.

Bundy was backed by his prominent Establishment family, which included brother McGeorge Bundy, later to be President Kennedy's national security advisor.

When McCarthy tried to subpoena Bundy to appear before his subcommittee, Dulles decided to take him on and make the fight public. In a July 9, 1953, speech on the Senate floor, McCarthy denounced Dulles for his "blatant attempt to thwart the authority of the Senate" and demanded that Dulles appear before the subcommittee.

Instead of continuing the public spat, Dulles came to McCarthy's office for a private meeting to explain his position. Citing the secret and sensitive nature of the CIA's mission, Dulles asked to be given immunity from congressional investigations.

Early in his investigation, McCarthy zeroed in on Cord Meyer at the CIA after receiving information from the FBI regarding Meyer's past associations with left-wing organizations.

A decorated marine in World War II who suffered serious injuries during combat, including the loss of his left eye, Meyer left the service with very strong anti-war views.

He cofounded the United World Federalists in 1947 with James Warburg of the Warburg banking dynasty to further the idea of a one world global state. The Warburg family was closely linked to President Franklin Roosevelt.

Warburg was a major proponent of the Morgenthau Plan to turn Germany into a nonindustrial, agrarian state as punishment for World War II. Secretary of the Navy James Forrestal, a leading critic of the Morgenthau Plan, would ultimately learn the heavy price of opposing these powers behind the scenes.

Meyer was backed by his wealthy family in his endeavors and served as a special assistant in the US delegation that helped to create the United Nations in 1945. A prominent leader in that delegation was Alger Hiss, who served as acting temporary secretary-general of the United Nations Charter Conference in San Francisco.

In August 1953, Meyer came under suspicion by the FBI, which informed the CIA it wouldn't give Meyer a security clearance. McCarthy was aware of the FBI stance. It heightened his interest in looking into communist infiltration of the intelligence community. Both CIA director Dulles and Richard Helms, Wisner's deputy in the OPC, stepped up to defend Meyer and block any FBI interrogation of Meyer.

Part of what triggered the FBI's concerns was Meyer's membership in various liberal organizations that the FBI considered "subversive."

At the same time, Dulles prevailed upon Wisner to get his media allies and stooges in Operation Mockingbird to begin their effort to undermine and destroy the Wisconsin senator. Operation Mockingbird was the CIA program to co-opt leading media figures and use them to disseminate CIA propaganda. Falling in line with derogatory columns and broadcast programs were such media luminaries as Edward Murrow, Drew Pearson, Joseph Alsop, Walter Lippman, and Ben Bradlee.

Part and parcel of the media subterfuge was an effort to smear McCarthy as a drunk and homosexual. The CIA offensive boosted morale internally and emboldened political figures in both parties to move against McCarthy, ultimately leading to his censure.

Disappointed by the failure to penetrate the media and political shield around the CIA, McCarthy still harbored the desire to expose what he felt was a serious Communist infiltration of the spy agency.

In March 1954, his subcommittee held a hearing regarding "alleged threats against the chairman." William Morgan, a military intelligence officer who had worked for C. D. Jackson in the White House, recalled a conversation with a CIA employee named Horace Craig.

Jackson ran a special psychological warfare program for President Eisenhower and would later surface as a leading figure in the *Time-Life* media empire. Ironically, Jackson would purchase the Zapruder film of the Kennedy assassination on behalf of *Life Magazine*.

Morgan alleged that Craig stated, "It may be necessary for liquidating Senator McCarthy as was Huey Long [Louisiana Governor assassinated in 1935]. There is always some madman who will do it for a price."

Little did the committee members appreciate the foreshadowing of McCarthy's ultimate fate. Certainly McCarthy's enemies in the CIA kept a wary eye on him, knowing that a wounded bear can be a serious threat at any time.

As we know from the work of many diligent researchers, there is more than reasonable suspicion to think some elements of the CIA could have been involved in the assassination of John F. Kennedy.

Among those CIA operatives more commonly mentioned as potential plotters are Allen Dulles, Cord Meyer, David Atlee Phillips, William Harvey, and David Morales. Also mentioned as likely being on the scene in Dallas on November 22, 1963, were Frank Sturgis, Eugenio Martinez, and Howard Hunt of Watergate burglar fame. Equal scrutiny should focus on longtime CIA hands like James Angleton and Richard Helms and what they may have known and covered up.

Had Joe McCarthy been able to pursue his investigation into possible CIA infiltrators to its fullest extent, President Kennedy might have not been assassinated on November 22, 1963. The senator's surprising death at Bethesda on May 2, 1957, freed the CIA from the intense scrutiny it fought so hard to deflect and shielded those in the Deep State with questionable loyalties from being revealed.

CHAPTER 8

JFK Autopsy Masks the True
Wounds Witnessed by Many

———

FOR MORE THAN FIFTY YEARS, the assassination of President John F. Kennedy has been billed the "crime of the century." Apart from the shooting itself, the immediate aftermath and autopsy performed at the Bethesda Naval Medical Center are part and parcel of that "crime of the century."

The formally accepted autopsy and its central role in the conclusions reached by the Warren Commission demonstrate a sinister effort to shield the truth of President Kennedy's murder from the American people.

An honest official assessment of all the president's wounds has been withheld. The final autopsy is backed up with some photographs that are clearly faked, crude forgeries that try to substantiate the "lone nut gunman" thesis immediately seized on by President Lyndon Johnson and his cohorts, including FBI director J. Edgar Hoover.

The immediate problem they had was trying to square the president's wounds with the scenario they were promoting. The other difficulty was reconciling the testimony of the doctors and nurses who attended to JFK immediately after the shooting with what the pathologists would report in their autopsy.

JFK sustained a horrific head wound that almost immediately proved fatal. By the time he arrived at Parkland Hospital just eight minutes after the shooting, he was essentially DOA. The attending physicians there immediately noted two primary wounds:

1. What appeared to be an entrance wound in the throat just below the Adam's apple
2. A massive head wound with entrance near the right temple, which resulted in an "avulsive" exit wound in the right rear of his head, producing a substantial loss of blood and brain matter

Given the immediacy of dealing with the head wound and trying to open an airway for the president, the doctors were not aware of a gunshot wound in JFK's back.

To the staff at Parkland Hospital, it was readily apparent that the shots that killed John Kennedy came from in front of him.

Dr. Robert McClelland was one of the first senior physicians to attend to the mortally wounded president. Some time afterward, he drew a sketch of the wounds he observed on the president's body.

The sketch, which remained hidden in the hands of a private collector for years, went on sale in June 2017 through an auction house, Nate D. Sanders Auctions in Los Angeles. It sold that month for $9,816.

The drawing clearly shows an entrance wound on the right temple above JFK's eye and a large four-by-five-inch exit wound at the right rear of the head.

It also depicts a small (six millimeter) "probable" entrance wound "low in the neck." On the sketch, McClelland notes a back wound that he didn't see but speculated was an exit wound in the undated but signed sketch.

In subsequent media interviews over the years, McClelland has been adamant about the gaping hole in the right rear of the president's head. In one, he noted that he looked at the hole "from 18 inches for about 12 minutes." He's described it as being the size of an orange. Not a sight you'd be likely to forget.

In an interview with the *Richmond Times-Dispatch*, published November 17, 2013, he clearly indicated his belief in at least two shooters carrying out the assassination. "The first bullet hit him in the back, not in the front as we thought at the time," he said. "Several seconds later, the second shot hits him and his head literally explodes, and he was thrown violently backward and to the left as you would expect someone hit by a high-caliber bullet from the front, not from above and behind."

When asked where he thought the shot had been fired, he said "It would have had to come in from the picket fence on the grassy knoll, in my view of it." A surgeon who'd treated many bullet wounds throughout his long medical career, McClelland firmly believed the second bullet hit Kennedy from the front and that the gaping hole he saw in the back of the head was clearly an exit wound.

The description of the head wound and the massive hole at the lower right portion of JFK's head was echoed by Secret Service agent Clint Hill, the first agent to respond to the shooting by getting onto the back of the limousine and helping Jacqueline Kennedy into the back seat after she tried to retrieve something from the top of the trunk, most likely a piece of JFK's skull that was blown out by the fatal head shot.

In a car behind the presidential limousine were reporters from the news wire services. Merriman Smith of *United Press International* (*UPI*) reported the wire car (car carrying reporters from the *Associated*

Press and *UPI*) arrived at Parkland Hospital just after the limousine. Smith dashed up to the president's limo to see what had happened.

He recalled, "I could see the blood spattered around the interior of the rear seat and a dark stain spreading down the president's dark gray suit." He noted Mrs. Kennedy was cradling the president's head and "was bent over as if she was whispering to him."

Smith then turned to Secret Service agent Hill and asked, "How badly was he hit, Clint?"

Hill replied, "He's dead, Smitty."

The official autopsy photographs do not depict anything remotely resembling such a devastating exit wound in the right rear of the head.

Equally troubling is how the autopsy handled the examination of the president's brain, which sustained such a horrific wound. From the Zapruder film, which captured the impact of the head shot, it is obvious that large portions of JFK's skull and brain were blown away from his head.

Yet the official photographs released publicly show no deformities to the head, and photographs of the brain allegedly removed from JFK's skull show an organ that is virtually intact.

The wounds as described in the official autopsy report, submitted finally on a third draft, include the following:

1. A bullet hole in the back, almost six inches below the right shoulder and to the right of the spinal column. There was no related exit wound for this shot and no bullet located.

2. An entry wound in the upper rear of the head and then what appeared to be an exit wound over the right ear toward the right temple.

3. The throat wound, which had been obliterated by a tracheotomy performed at Parkland to open an airway, was explained as a possible exit wound for the shot in the back. The final Warren Commission report was changed by commission member Gerald Ford, who moved the location of the back wound higher to make it support the single bullet theory.

The autopsy then was used to support the thesis that Lee Harvey Oswald fired three shots at the president, with one hitting JFK and then magically striking Texas governor John Connally, one bullet missing altogether, and then the final, fatal headshot.

A forest of trees has been felled for books that have torn the single bullet theory apart as preposterous and anatomically impossible. In addition, the ability of any marksman, let alone Oswald, to get off three shots from a bolt action rifle in such a short time frame (around six seconds) with high accuracy is ludicrous. Marine corps records indicate that Oswald was an average marksman at best.

What stands out as the more likely possibility is that President Kennedy was hit by possibly four bullets: one in the throat, one in the back, and two simultaneous shots to the head. That would leave a separate bullet or bullets for the wounds to Gov. Connally and at least three other stray shots that struck in and outside the limousine.

Until the day he died, John Connally insisted he was struck by a bullet separate from the one that hit JFK.

The discrepancy points to the likelihood of up to eight shots or more fired from at least two shooters from the rear and likely one or more from the front. JFK and Connally were caught in a deadly crossfire of bullets.

As with other criminal events that occurred at Bethesda (the Forrestal and McCarthy murders), another aspect that bears examination is the actual timeline of events.

Those of us watching the horrible events unfold that day on television can recall the scene of Air Force One arriving back in Washington and the president's casket being loaded into a *gray* navy ambulance.

Here is where the timeline gets very interesting.

An official log kept at Bethesda by Marine Sgt. Roger Boyajian recorded a *black* hearse arriving with the president's casket at 1835 military time (6:35 p.m.).

Between 6:40 and 6:45 p.m., Navy Petty Officer Dennis David, serving as the chief of the day for the medical school at Bethesda, gathered a group of sailors at the morgue loading dock, at the request of Secret Service agents, to carry a cheap, unadorned gray aluminum shipping casket from the *black* hearse into the morgue.

In a later conversation with Dr. Thornton Boswell (one of two pathologists who conducted the autopsy), David received confirmation that the president's body had been inside the shipping casket. Several of those present at the time recall removing the president's body from a zippered body bag.

When the president's body had been removed from Parkland Hospital for transport back to Washington, DC, it had been wrapped in two sheets, one around the body and the other around the head before being placed in a bronze casket. Testimony by Aubrey Rike, driver for O'Neal's Funeral Home and Ambulance Service, confirms that.

Meanwhile, at 6:55 p.m. the *gray* navy ambulance with the bronze casket arrived in front of the main building at Bethesda. Then, at around 7:17 p.m., the hearse traveled to the back of the morgue, where FBI agents James Sibert and Francis O'Neill, along with two Secret Service agents, used a dolly to move the bronze casket into the morgue.

The autopsy of John F. Kennedy then allegedly began at 8:15 p.m. with a Y-incision in his chest.

The lingering question regarding the events at Bethesda on November 22, 1963, is this: In the period between the arrival of the body at 6:35 p.m. and the beginning of the autopsy at 8:15 p.m., were there steps taken to alter the body and cover up the original status of the wounds suffered by John F. Kennedy? Or were the pathologists coached in what to report, regardless of what they actually saw?

If so, then we have another treasonous crime of the highest order committed at Bethesda Naval Hospital, where Kennedy's mentor James Forrestal and good friend Joe McCarthy were earlier murdered.

CHAPTER 9

How Were JFK's Wounds Altered or Hidden?

———

LOOKING AT THE STATEMENTS OF the doctors first attending to the mortally wounded president and then reviewing the conclusions in the final autopsy report, it's all too evident that John F. Kennedy's wounds were ignored or altered at the Naval Medical Center in Bethesda on the evening of November 22, 1963, and that the final autopsy report was falsified.

As noted earlier, the doctors and other personnel at Parkland Hospital in Dallas were preoccupied with two wounds: the apparent entry wound in the throat below the Adam's apple and the gunshot to the head, which appeared to enter around the right temple.

No notice was made of the wound in the president's back about six inches below the shoulder and to the right of the spine.

The autopsy report finalized by Dr. James Humes and Dr. Thornton Boswell centered on a wound in the upper right center of the head that exited above JFK's right ear. Because of the intervention of Gerald Ford, the Warren Commission report placed the back wound five and a half inches higher in order to line it up with the neck wound, which it termed an exit wound as part of the infamous "magic bullet" theory.

No mention was made of the large exit wound in the lower right rear of the president's head witnessed by Secret Service agents and medical personnel in Dallas, key people at Bethesda including FBI agents, and the embalmer at the Washington funeral home where JFK's body was prepared for burial.

At Parkland Hospital, doctors Malcolm Perry, Kemp Clark, Robert McClelland, Ronald Jones, Paul Peters, and James Carrico, along with nurses and other medical personnel, all described the exit wound in the right rear of the head virtually identically.

This same wound was seen by Secret Service agents Clint Hill, Roy Kellerman, and William Greer, as well as by Admiral George Burkley, the president's personal physician, who was present at the autopsy as well, in addition to being at Parkland Hospital.

FBI agents Francis O'Neill and James Sibert, who helped move JFK's body into the Bethesda morgue, also noted the gaping exit wound in the right rear of the head while present at the autopsy.

As part of their duties, O'Neill and Sibert wrote up a report on what they did and witnessed at the JFK autopsy. The FD-302 report was dated November 26, 1963, and included sketches both agents made depicting the wounds they witnessed on the president's body.

Both men's sketches clearly show the massive wound in the right rear of JFK's head. The report remained classified at the time of the Warren Commission investigation.

Based on what they witnessed, particularly regarding the back wound, both agents totally discounted the single bullet theory, knowing it did not reflect the truth. Because it was known their report would not support the preposterous theory, neither agent was called to testify before the Commission, despite being credible eye-witnesses to the autopsy.

Thomas Evan Robinson was the embalmer at Gawler's Funeral Home in Washington, DC, who worked on the president's body to prepare it for burial after the autopsy was concluded. In an interview with JFK researcher Joe West on May 26, 1992, he noted the following observations of the wounds:

- Large, gaping hole in back of head, patched by placing a piece of rubber over it
- Skull filled with plaster of paris
- Smaller wound in right temple, crescent shaped, flapped down three inches
- Two small shrapnel wounds in the face packed with wax
- Wound in back, five to six inches below shoulder to the right of spine
- Adrenal gland and brain removed
- No swelling or discoloration in face due to instant death

Robinson's recollection is consistent with what the main doctors at Parkland reported with the exception that no mention was made of the neck wound, which had been significantly altered by the tracheotomy yet would have been covered up by clothing anyway for the burial.

These observations are supported as well by one of the autopsy technicians present at Bethesda that evening: Paul O'Connor.

O'Connor enlisted in the US Navy in 1959 and was subsequently stationed at Guantanamo Bay in Cuba. He returned to the United States and went for training to the Medical Technology School at the National Naval Medical Center in Bethesda.

As part of his training, he was assigned to the pathology department. During that period he assisted in more than sixty autopsies. In 2005, he was interviewed by William Matson Law for his book *In the Eye of History: Disclosures in the JFK Assassination Medical Evidence.*

O'Connor noted that the wound to the head was so massive that there was very little of the brain left to remove. He described the cranium as "shattered" and "totally fractured." He went on to add more detail as to the horrific effects of the gunshot.

"His right eye, as I remember, was poked completely out of the orbit, the eye casing," he said. "I remember that Dr. Boswell and I looked into the back of the cranium, looking towards the front, and the orbit—the bony casing around where the eye sits was completely fractured."

O'Connor related that at the start of the autopsy, the first task was to weigh and measure the body. When the body was finally turned over, the entrance bullet wound in the back was discovered on the right side of spinal column, around the location of the seventh vertebra. He recalled that the autopsy team was quite surprised to find the wound.

He said that Dr. Humes, the lead pathologist, poked his finger into the hole and said it didn't go anywhere, meaning the bullet had not penetrated very far into the body.

According to O'Connor, Dr. Pierre Finck, a forensic pathologist at the Armed Forces Institute of Pathology at Walter Reed Army Hospital, strenuously objected to what Commander Humes had done with the back wound.

Using a malleable probe, the autopsy doctors were able to establish their belief that the bullet entered the back, went through the muscles between the ribs, arched downward, hit the back of the pleural cavity, which encases the lungs, and stopped.

O'Connor said that as the autopsy was proceeding, the team was informed that the shots came from a high building. He explained that "meant the bullet had to be traveling in a downward trajectory, and we also realized that this bullet—that hit him in the back—is what we called in the military a 'short shot,' which means that the powder in the bullet was defective so it didn't have the power to push the projectile—the bullet—clear though the body. If it had been a full shot at the angle he was shot, it would have come out through his heart and through his sternum."

At Parkland Hospital on the day of the shooting, an intact bullet was found on a gurney that may have held President Kennedy. Speculation is that the bullet could have come out of the back wound when doctors attempted to externally massage JFK's heart.

The Warren Report identified that bullet as the miraculous "single bullet" that went through Kennedy and then Connally. Given the damage done to both men and the impact the bullet would have had with bones, there is no likelihood of it remaining intact and not fragmenting. So much for Arlen Specter's totally ridiculous single bullet theory of that one bullet striking both President Kennedy and Governor Connally.

It also proves the corruption of the Warren Commission and Gerald Ford in moving the location of the back wound to fit its theory, even knowing how many people had observed the real location.

Another critical question is what happened to the bullet that hit the president just below the Adam's apple in a shot fired from in front of him. No bullet was reported found in the body and there was no obvious sign of an exit wound.

As quoted in the *New York Times* of November 27, 1963, Dr. Kemp Clark of Parkland Hospital theorized that the bullet hit Kennedy right at the necktie knot and then "ranged downward in his chest, and did not exit." Another physician, Dr. Robert Shaw, supported this possibility in a *New York Herald Tribune* article on the same day by saying the bullet "coursed downward into his lung [and] was removed in the Bethesda Naval Hospital where the autopsy was performed."

These descriptions lend some credence to a bullet being fired from an elevated position in front of JFK, quite possibly the grassy knoll or picket fence often cited by assassination researchers.

FBI agents O'Neill and Sibert, who were present at the autopsy, noted in a letter dated November 22, 1963, "We hereby acknowledge receipt of a missile removed by Commander James J. Humes, MC, USN on this date."

Interestingly enough, a letter dated November 26, 1963, from the Protective Research Section of the Treasury Department said it received from Dr. Burkley the receipt from the FBI "for a missile removed during physical examination of the body." Did this refer to the O'Neill and Sibert letter, or was yet another bullet recovered?

A key factor in the president's wounds was the back brace he wore that day. His actions during the PT 109 incident only served to aggravate an already bad back condition. As he got older, the back trouble that plagued him most of his adult life required the brace be worn on public occasions at a minimum. It's likely that the first shots before the fatal headshot would have caused him to fall to the floor of the limousine. But the brace kept him upright enough to be struck by the fatal head shot.

In terms of the massive head wound, O'Connor noted, "It looked to me like a bomb had exploded inside his brain and blew out the whole side of his head. I've never seen a more horrendous destruction of the cranium, unless it was done by a very high-caliber weapon. I found out later it was done by a Mannlicher Carcano—a cheap Italian rifle—just about what I would call a thirty caliber or thirty-thirty caliber rifle."

O'Connor told William Matson Law in no uncertain terms he could not believe that a Mannlicher Carcano rifle was capable of inflicting the kind of damage he saw. The copper jacketed ammunition purportedly used by the alleged assassin Oswald would not have caused the massive damage seen inside the president's head. The many bullet fragments found within the cranium indicate an explosive bullet that fragmented upon striking the target.

As it turns out, years later O'Connor would learn more about the events of November 22 that would explain the odd things he observed at the JFK autopsy. Immediately following the autopsy, he and others who participated in the autopsy were instructed they were never to discuss the events of that evening and were forced to sign orders of silence under penalty of general court martial.

As a loyal navy medical corpsman who valued his career, O'Connor followed orders and kept his mouth shut. In 1965 he was assigned to the US Marine Corps in Vietnam, where he was wounded and eventually medically discharged.

After his discharge, he realized the threats issued in the aftermath of the autopsy would no longer carry any weight.

Some time afterward, in the late seventies or early eighties, O'Connor had the opportunity to attend a conference under the invitation of noted JFK researcher David Lifton and meet some of the doctors from Parkland Hospital who attended to JFK.

As a result of those discussions, O'Connor learned about the entry wound in the throat that had been dismissed as a botched tracheotomy by the team at Bethesda.

What really stunned him was the revelation that the president's body had been placed in a bed liner before being removed from Parkland Hospital in an expensive bronze casket.

O'Connor recalled being on duty when JFK's body arrived in an aluminum shipping casket at the Bethesda morgue. Upon opening that casket, the Bethesda team found the president's body in a body bag with nothing wrapped around his torso as some recall at

Parkland when the body was awaiting pickup by the ambulance from the O'Neal Funeral Home for transport to Air Force One at Love Field in Dallas. O'Connor did recall that there was a sheet wrapped around JFK's head covering the wounds. Was the president's body moved from one casket to another while in transit?

Another strange aspect of the autopsy was described by Dennis David, chief petty officer who served as chief of the day on November 22. That evening he was asked to type a memo for an FBI agent that said four bullet fragments had been removed from President Kennedy's head during the autopsy. Was this memo different from the missile receipt letter?

A few days later, David went to see Lieutenant Commander William Pitzer, head of the audio and visual department at the Bethesda Medical School. He found him working on a 16-mm film, slides, and black-and-white photos of the Kennedy autopsy. David noted the materials showed what appeared to be an entry wound in the right frontal area of the head and a corresponding exit wound in the lower rear of the skull.

Although Pitzer was not present at the autopsy, it's known that the hospital had a closed-circuit television system that made it possible to film the morgue for instructional movies. Did Pitzer, in fact, secretly film the Kennedy autopsy?

David recalls seeing both color and black-and-white prints of the autopsy. He noted the photos showed a small entry wound on the right side of the forehead and a larger exit wound in the right rear of the head. Such photos would be indisputable proof of a conspiracy involving multiple shooters and a falsified autopsy.

Pitzer never shared his film and photographs with anyone. As he was getting ready to retire in 1966, he was found dead in his office with a gunshot wound to the right temple. There were no powder burns around the wound, but navy investigators and the FBI ultimately concluded the wound was self-inflicted.

David and others could testify that Pitzer was left-handed, making such a shot to the right temple impossible. Because of the lack of powder burns around the wound, the shot had to have come from a distance of about three feet.

The Pitzer film and photographs have never surfaced. Thus, how the "crime of the century" transpired in Dallas was hidden by a major crime of its own in Bethesda and a subsequent cover-up.

CHAPTER 10

Bethesda Events Profoundly Changed American History

———

WITHIN THE SPACE OF FOURTEEN years, American history was drastically altered by the treachery and betrayals occurring at the National Naval Medical Center in Bethesda, Maryland.

When casually driving by the facility and looking at the iconic tower, one has no idea of the criminal acts perpetrated there. But we've certainly felt the effects ever since.

The death of James Forrestal proved there were forces within our country and government that couldn't tolerate a true patriot taking on global communism. Perhaps it was then that the Deep State first reared its ugly head, although some observers believe General George Patton may have been its first victim.

The rapid rise of Joe McCarthy to prominence and the far-reaching impact of his crusade against Communists in government and our leading academic, media, and cultural institutions produced a backlash that ended with the destruction of a great American's career and life.

As he gained public acclaim and generated genuine devotion on the part of many Americans, Jack Kennedy frightened the behind-the-scenes powers who recognized his reelection would greatly strengthen his hand in rooting out those who were trying to block his agenda's progress and those who did not put our nation's interests first.

The shocking and brutal assassination of a beloved president opened a wound in the national psyche that's never healed. For many of us alive then, November 22, 1963, was the day America died.

There would be no turning back to the halcyon life of the 1950s and early 1960s. America was prosperous, civil rights were being extended to all Americans, and we were exploring a new frontier on our way to the moon.

But for those who consolidated their power through the betrayals at Bethesda, there were threats that remained. Disenchantment with the Vietnam War and its prosecution by the Johnson administration started new political movements that concerned the Establishment.

What really played on the mind of President Lyndon Johnson, as he pondered a run for reelection in 1968, was the ultimate wild card: Senator Robert F. Kennedy of New York, his predecessor's brother.

At the same time, the Reverend Dr. Martin Luther King had created a national civil rights movement that engaged Americans of all races and economic backgrounds.

King's "I Have a Dream" speech on August 28, 1963, at the Lincoln Memorial gave him a truly national following and stature as a major political figure. What really caught the attention of the DC elite was his stated opposition to the Vietnam War.

Not liking the hand he'd been dealt by rapidly changing events, LBJ decided to forego another term as president, announcing he would not seek reelection in 1968. The unlikely rise of Senator Eugene McCarthy as a contender for the Democratic presidential nomination and the expected bid of Vice President Hubert Humphrey for the top prize opened the door for a new contender who would capture the public's imagination: Bobby Kennedy.

For the Bethesda betrayers, the prospect of RFK as president was unacceptable. He was the type of man who would no doubt launch an effort to uncover the truth regarding his brother's murder and even possibly look into the death of his good friend and mentor Joe McCarthy.

Complicating that scenario was the real prospect that Dr. King might endorse Bobby Kennedy's presidential bid, which would likely guarantee his nomination and ultimate election to the White House.

We all know too well what happened in April and June 1968: these two crusading figures met violent and untimely deaths at the hands of assassins.

As was the case with President Kennedy, both murders were attributed to lone gunmen. But as is the case of both crimes, as well as the JFK assassination, the "lone nut gunman" theory simply does not hold up under serious scrutiny.

Here is a brief analysis of where both cases against James Earl Ray and Sirhan Sirhan break down:

MARTIN LUTHER KING MURDER IN MEMPHIS, APRIL 4, 1968

As we know, petty criminal James Earl Ray was charged with the murder of Dr. King, who was killed by a single rifle shot to the head. Ray confessed to the crime in order to avoid the death penalty, but later tried unsuccessfully to change his plea and get a real trial.

The shot that killed Dr. King was obviously fired by an expert marksman, most likely a military-trained sniper, which Ray was not. The bullet struck Dr. King in the jaw, traveled downward and severed his spinal cord. He was essentially dead before he hit the floor of the motel balcony.

The window from which Ray allegedly fired the shot did not provide a clear view of the target and would involve the shooter firing from a very awkward position.

From an analysis of photographs from the scene, those standing with Dr. King on the motel balcony pointed in the direction of a bushy hillside next to the rooming house where Ray supposedly fired the shot.

Ray was obviously involved in a conspiracy, as evidenced by his circuitous escape through Canada to Europe. He clearly had help to get out of the country, but also was set up as the patsy.

ROBERT KENNEDY MURDER IN LOS ANGELES, JUNE 5, 1968

After winning the California primary and giving a rousing victory speech, Bobby Kennedy left the ballroom and headed through the kitchen area to another part of the Ambassador Hotel for a press conference.

There, in the kitchen pantry, Sirhan Sirhan began firing with his pistol as the Kennedy party approached. Sirhan fired eight shots from his revolver as Kennedy walked right in front of him.

None of the shots actually hit Senator Kennedy. Five members of the Kennedy party were wounded by the Sirhan shots.

RFK suffered three wounds, all of which were fired from behind him. One bullet struck him in the right rear armpit and did not exit. Another shot hit him in the same area and exited through his chest. The third wound was a fatal shot to the head. A fourth shot went through the right shoulder of his jacket without hitting him.

His mortal head wound was the result of a shot fired from about two inches behind him, hitting the base of his skull behind his right ear.

Once again, a Kennedy had been slain with a fatal shot to the head.

One has to wonder if Sirhan was meant as a decoy to draw attention his way while the real assassin delivered the fatal shot to Kennedy. Was Sirhan simply the patsy?

Those hit, including Kennedy, were struck by ten bullets alleged to have been fired by Sirhan from an eight-round revolver. Without a doubt, there was a second shooter who got away with the murder of Bobby Kennedy.

Both the King and Kennedy cases merit greater attention and investigation beyond what we review here. The betrayals set in motion at Bethesda continued well into the latter part of the 1960s and beyond. The attempted assassinations of George Wallace and Ronald Reagan had strange aspects to them as well.

Violent events shaping politics is not peculiar to America. History in general tells us a lot about human nature, the thirst some have for power over others, and the betrayals they will commit to reach their ends.

The lessons we can draw from the betrayal at Bethesda are that we must never take our freedoms for granted. People must be held accountable for their crimes, no matter how powerful. Certainly that's an issue that confronts our society today.

James Forrestal, Joe McCarthy, and Jack Kennedy deserve no less than for that accountability to eventually come true. Those who committed those vile deeds may be dead, but history must demand the truth be revealed to prevent evil, power-mad individuals from triumphing over what is right and good.

AFTERWORD: OUR CAUSE LIVES ON: FIGHTING THE DEEP STATE AND THE FORCES OF EVIL

——

WITH THE HISTORIC ELECTION OF Donald Trump as the forty-fifth president of the United States behind us, it's readily apparent that the United States continues to face its most dangerous period in history: if the forces of globalism, the New World Order, and the Deep State conspire to thwart the Trump administration's nationalist, populist movement, our democratic republic will become even more threatened.

The incredible inroads that global communism made in transforming the United States of America since the days of the New Deal is approaching a point where it may not be reversed.

Our major institutions are dominated by left-leaning ideologues, from academia, journalism, entertainment, and religion to even the bulwarks of capitalism, where slavish devotion to political correctness, multiculturalism, and diversity has undermined traditional American values of patriotism, individual responsibility, merit, and national unity.

James Forrestal, Joe McCarthy, and Jack Kennedy would be appalled to see how the democratic republic they served so devotedly is coming undone by the emergence of the Uniparty, a DC elite that thrives on influence and corruption. What we have is Progressive Fascism and the Deep State that seeks to crush all who oppose it.

Globalists led by former Nazi collaborator and multibillionaire George Soros seek "open borders" by which a wealthy elite will control economies and dictate how people shall live.

Donald Trump articulated the most pressing issue of our time: Any nation without borders is no longer a nation. A country that won't and can't defend itself from invasion or infiltration will eventually fall to outsiders in league with treasonous insiders. He knows all too well the time is right to put America first.

The flood of bogus "refugees" into America is designed to wipe out the last vestiges of the America we know and love. As instructed by Soros and other globalist masters, Barack Obama and Hillary Clinton opened the gates for Islamists and Latin Americans to carry out the transformation that will end the American way of life as we know it.

Sure, prominent politicians and cultural figures still pay lip service to American exceptionalism and religious freedom. But with the entrenchment of the abortion industry and its subsidization by taxpayers, America has unwittingly embraced a practice that may ultimately lead to its demise.

A nation that kills its infants in utero is one that mocks God and his greatest creation, life itself. Such a nation cannot endure under the weight of such evil and sin. Thankfully, there are encouraging signs that younger Americans are taking a second look at this horrible practice, which began as genocide against black Americans and the disabled. We must become a nation that is truly pro-life in every way if the United States is to survive.

Progressive Fascists also want to end our Second Amendment rights, because a nation whose citizens are unarmed is one that can be completely subjected to totalitarianism, a fact Adolf Hitler knew all too well.

So, what are we to do? We must reject the notion that American nationalism is wrong. We must insist we remain free to defend it at the grassroots level with our God-given right to bear arms. We don't need government permission to defend ourselves, our families, and our property.

We also must insist our educational system return to a balanced curriculum that encourages an exchange of ideas without the conformist restrictions imposed by cultural Marxists. We need to end the indoctrination that passes for education in our government schools at every level.

The silent majority is silent no more. Its voice shattered the Establishment's complacency on November 8, 2016. We must continue to speak up and speak out vociferously. We have to reject the epithets and smears Progressive Fascists use to make people toe the Party line. By calling Donald Trump, conservatives, and Trump supporters "racist," they render the term utterly meaningless.

James Forrestal, Joe McCarthy, and Jack Kennedy were entirely right about the global menace posed by communism. They were right to try to root out those who wanted to undermine and transform the American way of life and totally denigrate traditional American values.

They paid for their devotion to the United States with their lives. The forces behind those heinous crimes may never be conclusively identified. But we will keep trying to set the historical record straight, no matter how distasteful that truth might be.

Clearly there were forces within the American government that wanted to subvert the policies these three men worked so tirelessly to implement and promote. Those forces still exist today.

This treachery began in the wake of the Depression and continues as Progressive Fascists advance the myths of McCarthyism, continuing to smear those who share the Forrestal-McCarthy-Kennedy vision for America.

Our cause is just. It must thrive and live on into the next generation. Those who carry its banner know how hard Progressive Fascists will fight to continue their single-minded quest to destroy American values, promote godless secularism, and embrace an elitist, globalist vision that will mean the end of the United States of America as we know and love it.

They underestimate what we bring to the battlefield. Inspired by the courage and commitment of James Forrestal, Joe McCarthy, and Jack Kennedy, we have the strength, moral fortitude, and patriotic duty to preserve and expand their great legacy. Donald Trump's victory shows the momentum has swung our way.

This marks the end of *Betrayal at Bethesda*. But it signifies the continuance of a long struggle to defeat and destroy the truly evil Deep State forces we fight. More research is underway to further reveal the treachery that's enveloped our beloved land for almost a century. What's coming is easily as shocking as what you've just read.

May God give us the strength to carry the battle forward, and may many patriots join us as well.

J. C. Hawkins
St. Augustine, Florida

THIS COMPILATION IS BASED ON *previous research by a number of prominent authors and investigators, ranging from Herbert Hoover and Herbert Romerstein to Stanton Evans and Diana West, among others. It's also sourced from government documents.*

Grouped by Branch of Government to Show Depth of Penetration and Infiltration

Samuel Dickstein	US congressman, Democrat from Manhattan, New York City, 1923-45; then New York State Supreme Court justice
Linn Farish	Office of Strategic Services (OSS); forerunner organization of the Central Intelligence Agency (CIA); assigned to Tito's headquarters in Yugoslavia during World War II
Cora Dubois	OSS; then State Department

Maurice Halperin	OSS
Hans Hirschfeld	OSS
Aldo Icardi	OSS**
Julius Joseph	OSS, Far Eastern Section, focus on Japan
Philip Keeney	OSS; former Library of Congress; after OSS, Foreign Economic Administration, (husband of Mary Jane Keeney)
James Speyer Kronthal	OSS; then CIA
Duncan Lee	OSS, assistant to OSS director William Donovan
Carl LoDolce	OSS**
Leonard Mins	OSS, Russian Section; passed info to Soviet Military Intelligence (GRU) revealing US efforts to crack Soviet codes
Franz Neumann	OSS; then State Department
Helen Tenney	OSS, Spanish Section
George Zlatovski	OSS
Jane Foster Zlatovski	OSS
Edna Jerry Askwith	State Department, Inter-American Affairs
Esther Brunauer	State Department, worked for Alger Hiss in the Office of Special Political Affairs; discharged as a security risk in 1952 because of ties to her husband, Stephen Brunauer, who was forced to resign from the US Navy as a security risk
Lois Carlisle	State Department; former OSS

Edmund Clubb	State Department, consul general in China
Henry Collins	State Department
Laurence Duggan*	State Department, head of Latin American Division and personal advisor to Secretary Cordell Hull
Gustavo Duran	State Department, Office of the Coordinator of Inter-American Affairs; then special assistant to the assistant secretary of state; then United Nations
Francis Ferry	State Department; then CIA
Noel Field	State Department, West European Division; a committed Communist and spy for the Soviets who left State in the late 1930s to work for the League of Nations in Geneva.
Herbert Fierst	State Department
Irving Goldman	State Department; former OSS
Stanley Graze	State Department; then United Nations; former OSS
Joseph Gregg	State Department, Office of the Coordinator of Inter-American Affairs
Haldore Hanson	State Department
Alger Hiss*	State Department; then United Nations Founding Conference; he began his government career in 1933 as an attorney in the Justice Department; he moved to the State Department in 1936
Donald Hiss	State Department, aide to then Assistant Secretary Dean Acheson;

	then Department of Labor; (brother of Alger Hiss)
Victor Hunt	State Department
Philip Jessup	State Department, ambassador at large; authored "white paper" that advanced the cause of the Chinese Communists over the Chinese Nationalists
Mary Jane Keeney	State Department; then Bureau of Economic Warfare; then United Nations, (wife of Philip Keeney)
Dorothy Kenyon	State Department; appointed to United Nations Commission; former New York judge
Emmanuel Larsen	State Department; former Office of Naval Intelligence
Leander Lovell	State Department
Carl Marzani	State Department, handled preparation of top secret reports; former Works Progress Administration (WPA); then OSS prior to State Department; was member of the Communist Party USA before joining OSS
Peveril Meigs	State Department; then US Army; former OSS
Robert Miller	State Department, Office of the Coordinator of Inter-American Affairs
Edward Posniak	State Department; then International Monetary Fund
Richard Post	State Department

Bernard Redmont	State Department, head of News Division of the Office of the Coordinator of Inter-American Affairs; then journalist for *US News & World Report*; then dean of the Boston University School of Journalism
William Remington	State Department; then Department of Commerce, Natural Resources Planning Board; then War Production Board, chief of Export Control Division; then President's Council of Economic Advisers for FDR
Rowena Rommel	State Department
John Stewart Service	State Department, assigned to China as liaison with Communist Party leadership; roommate in China with Treasury official Solomon Adler (see below)
Harlow Shapley	State Department
John Carter Vincent	State Department, Office of Far Eastern Affairs
David Wahl	State Department, Office of Inter-American Affairs
David Weintraub	State Department; then United Nations, Office of Foreign Relief and Rehabilitation Operations
Frank White	State Department
David Zablodowsky	State Department; then United Nations, director of Publishing Division
Solomon Adler	US Treasury, Treasury representative to China (roommate of John

	Stewart Service in China); former State Department
Paul Appleby	US Treasury, Bureau of Budget; then Department of Agriculture, under secretary
Frank Coe	US Treasury, Bureau of Monetary Research
Sonia Gold	US Treasury
Irving Kaplan	US Treasury; then chief advisor to the Military Government of Germany
Victor Perlo	US Treasury; Office of Price Administration; War Production Board
Nathan Silvermaster (a.k.a. Gregory)	US Treasury; War Production Board
Harry Dexter White*	US Treasury, special assistant to Treasury Secretary Henry Morgenthau Jr.; then International Monetary Fund
John Abt	Department of Agriculture, Works Progress Administration (WPA); then Senate Committee on Education and Labor; then Justice Department
James Gorham	Department of Agriculture, WPA, Office of Price Administration
C.B. "Beanie" Baldwin	Department of Agriculture, Agricultural Adjustment Administration (AAA)
Stephen Brunauer	Department of Agriculture, research chemist; then US Naval Reserve, head of high explosives research for the Bureau of Naval Ordnance; then US Navy as

	civilian in Bureau of Naval Ordnance, resigned as accused security risk in 1951 because of his close association with known Soviet espionage agent Noel Field; (husband of Esther Brunauer)
Whittaker Chambers	Department of Agriculture (WPA)
Henry Collins	Department of Agriculture, National Recovery Administration (NRA)
Harold Glasser	Department of Agriculture; WPA; then US Treasury economic analyst
John Herrmann	Department of Agriculture, AAA
Harry Hopkins*	Department of Agriculture; then special assistant to President Franklin Roosevelt (Hopkins actually lived in the White House)
Charles Kramer	Department of Agriculture, AAA; then National Labor Relations Board
Lee Pressman	Department of Agriculture, WPA
Henry Julian Wadleigh	Department of Agriculture; then State Department
Harold Ware	Department of Agriculture
Nathaniel Weyl	Department of Agriculture, AAA; then Board of Economic Warfare (BEW)
Donald Wheeler	Department of Agriculture; then US Treasury; then OSS
Nathan Witt	Department of Agriculture; then National Labor Relations Board
Judith Coplon	Department of Justice; passed counterintelligence information to the Soviet Union

Theodore Geiger	Economic Cooperation Administration; former State Department
Thomas Arthur Bisson	Bureau of Economic Warfare, Asia specialist; then Institute of Pacific Relations (IPR)
Benjamin Cohn	White House counsel; then State Department counselor
Lauchlin Currie*	White House economic advisor to President Franklin Roosevelt; former US Treasury
David Demarest Lloyd	White House speechwriter; former State Department
David Niles	White House, assistant to Harry Hopkins; former WPA; former Department of Commerce
Michael Straight	White House speechwriter; then State Department, Eastern Division
Louis Adamic	Office of War Information, Yugoslav desk
James Aronson	Office of War Information
Julia Older Bazer	Office of War Information; handled cable file to Moscow; sister of Andrew Older, assistant to Drew Pearson, and FBI-confirmed Communist agent
Joseph Fels Barnes	Office of War Information (Eisenhower ghost writer for *Crusade in Europe*)
Cedric Belfrage	Office of War Information, de-Nazification team
John Fairbank	Office of War Information; former OSS; then Harvard University history

professor who advocated for recognition of the Chinese Communists as the legitimate government in the late 1940s

Paul Hagen — Office of War Information, German desk; close associate of White House economic advisor Lauchlin Currie and First Lady Eleanor Roosevelt

Travis Hendrick — Office of War Information

William Hinton — Office of War Information; strong booster of Chinese Communist Party

David Karr — Office of War Information; later assistant to columnist Drew Pearson; a later business associate of Armand Hammer

Robin Kinkead — Office of War Information

Owen Lattimore — Office of War Information, head of Pacific area

Irving Lerner — Office of War Information, Motion Picture Division

Philleo Nash — Office of War Information; then Truman White House

Carlo a Prato — Office of War Information, Italian desk

Peter Rhodes — Office of War Information, London office

Arthur Salman — Office of War Information, Poland desk

Flora Wovschin — Office of War Information; then State Department; renounced US citizenship after World War II and moved to Soviet Union

Charles W. Thayer	Head of Voice of America; former OSS
Edward Fitzgerald	Department of Commerce, War Production Board
Harry Magdoff	Department of Commerce, War Production Board
Herbert Fuchs	National Labor Relations Board; later professor of law at American University
George Shaw Wheeler	National Labor Relations Board
George Silverman	Railroad Retirement Board
Lewis Balamuth	Scientist, Manhattan Project
Edward Condon	Nuclear physicist, Los Alamos A-Bomb Project; then director, National Bureau of Standards
Robert Davis	Scientist, Los Alamos A-Bomb Project
Klaus Fuchs	Nuclear scientist, Los Alamos A-Bomb Project
Philip Morrison	Researcher, Los Alamos A-Bomb Project; then Atomic Energy Commission
J. Robert Oppenheimer,	Nuclear scientist, Los Alamos A-bomb Project
George Blake Charney	US Army
Kenneth Eckert	US Army
Stephen Fischer	US Army, Information and Education Division
David Greenglass	US Army; then Atomic Energy Commission; brother of Ethel Rosenberg, wife of convicted spy Julius Rosenberg
John Lautner	US Army Intelligence
William Martin	US Army

Marshall Wolfe	US Army; then State Department; then United Nations
Harriman Dash	Army Signal Corps
Peter Gragis	Army Signal Corps
Fred Kitty	Army Signal Corps engineer
Annie Lee Moss	Army Signal Corps
Julius Rosenberg	Army Signal Corps; the Atomic Energy Commission; executed in the electric chair, as was his wife Ethel, for passing atomic secrets to the Soviet Union; testimony from David Greenglass was critical to their conviction
William Weisbund	US Army Signal Security Agency; alerted Soviet Union that United States had cracked its code
William Perl	Department of the Navy
Isadore Amdur	Bureau of Naval Ordnance
Max Elitcher	Bureau of Naval Ordnance
Martin Sobell	Bureau of Naval Ordnance

This list conclusively confirms that James Forrestal and Joe McCarthy were correct about the infiltration of the US government by dedicated communists and their subsequent influence on US government policy.

While the penetration was widespread throughout the government, it was especially heavy in the State Department, the Office of Strategic Services, and the Office of War Information. It even included the higher echelons of the Roosevelt and Truman White Houses.

*Key officials who personally advised President Franklin D. Roosevelt and heavily influenced policies in favor of the Soviet Union. These individuals were among the worst traitors in American history.

** Icardi and LoDolce were both convicted by an Italian court in absentia for the murder of OSS major William Hollohan, allegedly done at the direction of Italian Communists.

———

Looking back over my life, I'm struck by events I experienced that intersected with principal actors and happenings related to Betrayal at Bethesda. *Somehow, I don't think they were totally random.*

Let me share those events, which ultimately laid the groundwork for this book. Like putting the pieces of a puzzle together, they seemed very much intertwined and connected. As my mother often said, "Things happen for a reason."

On October 12, 1962, I stood by the side of the road along the Ohio River Boulevard in Edgeworth, Pennsylvania, watching President John F. Kennedy pass by on his way to Pittsburgh, following a speech in Aliquippa. He was traveling in a Lincoln Continental convertible, sitting up in back waving to those lining the boulevard. Accompanying him were Governor David Lawrence and Senator Richardson Dilworth.

I was attending tenth grade social studies class at Quaker Valley High School in Leetsdale, Pennsylvania, on November 22, 1963, when our school learned from an intercom announcement that President Kennedy had been shot in Dallas. Shortly afterward, the entire school found out the president had died. With tears in our eyes, we were dismissed for the day.

On that same dark day in Dallas, Chuck Roberts, *Newsweek* White House correspondent, was in the press bus following President Kennedy's motorcade. (He later was my boss at the National Wildlife Federation in 1975–76 and a great mentor in the ways of Washington.)

Chuck was one of only two reporters allowed on Air Force One to witness the swearing in of Lyndon Johnson as president of the United States. In photographs of the ceremony, he can be seen in a rear doorway behind the presidential group. He later wrote a book defending the Warren Commission. (Chuck was the inspiration for the play and movie *Mr. Roberts*, which was written by his college roommate.)

Along with millions of Americans and millions of non-Americans around the world, on November 25, 1963, I watched in horror as Jack Ruby shot Lee Harvey Oswald on live television.

On November 19, 1965, for the first time, the thespians at Quaker Valley presented a dramatic play, *The Crucible* by Arthur Miller. I had the demanding lead role as John Proctor. At the time, I was totally unaware that Miller wrote the play as an attack on Joe McCarthy.

I left Quaker Valley in September 1966 and began my college days at Princeton University. One of the benefits of my education was the type of speakers who'd come to campus. In the fall of 1967, former CIA director Allen Dulles (and JFK foe) spoke at a politics seminar in which I participated. As I watched Dulles smoking his pipe, I felt something ominous, even sinister, about the man, who was a Princeton alumnus and trustee.

On April 4, 1968, Martin Luther King Jr. was assassinated in Memphis. Charlie Cleaves, a Shelby County deputy, was riding in a patrol car at the time of the shooting. He later told me the communications system went down for a while and those in patrol cars were unable to know what was happening. He believed the system failure was much more than a coincidence.

After I moved to Memphis in September 1995, Charlie became my best local friend, opening doors and introducing me to many in town. As tough as he was as a deputy, I never met a person with a bigger heart and more generous nature.

Throughout much of 1968, Charlie was one of the deputies assigned to the cell with accused King assassin James Earl Ray, watching him in a twelve-hour shift to prevent suicide or an attempt on Ray's life. Charlie shared with me his belief that Ray was incredibly ignorant and wholly incapable of plotting to kill Dr. King. He noted it was obvious Ray had to have help to escape to Europe. He later received many letters from Ray, who insisted on his innocence and that he was set up as a patsy.

(As a funny sidelight, Charlie related how guards would bring two meals to the cell, one for Ray and the other for the guard in the cell with him. Worried about the possibility of poisoning, Charlie wouldn't eat the meal. A big, strapping man, Charlie joked that he lost twenty pounds that year.)

In 1975–76, while working for the National Wildlife Federation and Chuck Roberts in Washington, my wife and I often attended noon Mass at St. Matthew's Cathedral, site of the funerals for Joe McCarthy and Jack Kennedy. We both worked in downtown, so it was an easy walk to meet up at lunchtime for Mass.

One final memory keeps coming back to me. In July 1969, as a member of the US Naval Reserve on a training mission, I served on the USS *Independence*, which was the backup recovery ship for Apollo 11, the first manned spacecraft to the moon, a mission fulfilling one of JFK's fondest dreams.

Out of all the ships to which I could have been assigned, I was sent to the fourth and final member of the *Forrestal* class of aircraft carriers. That mighty warship, CV-62, with its impressive air wing, certainly did its namesake proud.

Looking back on these various events and remarkable individuals, I now believe I was destined to write *Betrayal at Bethesda.* The benefit of all the experiences recalled here and their connections to three great American patriots certainly inspired me.

Beginning with seeing JFK in 1962, through working with Chuck Roberts (who greatly honed my writing skills), to becoming such a close friend to Charlie Cleaves, I sense a thread to my life. It's a thread tying together what first seemed like coincidences into a life's work that creates a fresh look at a troubled history that unfolded and continues to unfold before our eyes.

———

THIS BOOK REPRESENTS THE CULMINATION of years of research that's built on the heroic efforts of many patriotic Americans who've fought to preserve our freedom and economic liberty by digging for the truth.

The bibliography included with this book represents a library that interested readers should investigate to appreciate what's really happened in American history over the past eight decades.

Of special note are the following:

Medford and Stanton Evans—A father and son team of distinguished journalists whose landmark books are absolute must-reads on Senator Joseph McCarthy and the towering achievements he had in fighting global communism: *The Assassination of Joe McCarthy* (Medford) and *Blacklisted by History: The Untold History of Senator Joe McCarthy and His Fight against America's Enemies* (Stanton).

Herbert Romerstein—He teamed with **Stanton Evans** on *Stalin's Secret Agents: The Subversion of Roosevelt's Government*, as well as with **Eric Breindel** on *The Venona Secrets: Exposing Soviet Espionage and America's Traitors*, both incredible works of scholarship.

Dr. Paul Kengor—A Grove City College professor of history whose book *Dupes: How America's Adversaries Have Manipulated Progressives for a Century*, ripped the lid off the scandalous capitulation by leaders in government, academia, entertainment, and business to become "useful idiots" for global communism.

John Koster—His research for *Operation Snow: How a Soviet Mole in FDR's White House Triggered Pearl Harbor* uncovered the worst treason in American history.

Diana West—Her 2013 best seller, *American Betrayal: The Secret Assault on Our Nation's Character*, proved an inspirational source for me.

In addition, there are researchers who've published their own accounts on Internet websites that proved invaluable in uncovering important aspects of our recent history that have been hidden or obscured.

A special commendation goes to David Martin (DC Dave), a Washington economist and political commentator. His research into the death of James Forrestal led to public release of a report produced by a naval review board looking into the Forrestal death.

The Willcutts Report, as it is titled, was kept secret for fifty-five years until Martin finally got the judge advocate general for the US Navy to release it in 2004. Martin then provided it to the Seeley Mudd Manuscript Library of Princeton University, which is the repository of James Forrestal's official papers.

In addition to being an accomplished poet, Martin demonstrated serious investigative talents with his research into the Forrestal death and also the related death of Joe McCarthy at Bethesda as well.

As a young boy entering kindergarten, I was stricken with a serious illness—infectious hepatitis. It's believed I contracted the disease from an unsterilized needle used while I was part of the first select group of children being tested with the polio vaccine developed by Dr. Jonas Salk. I have memories of receiving injections from Dr. Salk, who was a kind man and scientific genius.

As a result, I spent much of the next seven or eight months virtually bedridden. I passed the time reading and doing jigsaw puzzles. I developed a real skill with puzzles. At age five, I was able to do the five-hundred-plus-piece puzzles created for adults. This activity taught me to be able to look at the "big picture" and see how things fit together.

I first began to synthesize the correlations among the fates of Forrestal, McCarthy, and Kennedy at Bethesda while in recovery from a cerebral aneurysm and hemorrhagic stroke in 2008–09. I survived thanks to the brilliant neurosurgeons and caring nursing staff at the University of Florida Shands Hospital in Gainesville. They are beyond world-class.

In addition to physical, speech, and occupational therapy, part of my recovery involved cognitive therapy at the Brooks Rehabilitation Hospital in Jacksonville.

The outstanding therapy received from the Brooks staff helped repair the damage from my stroke and had an incredible side benefit as well. After having my brain reenergized and trained to look at things in a different way while building an incredible memory, I found myself with a supercharged brain with new powers to analyze situations and see connections I never would've noticed before.

A major learning in this process was coming to the realization that there is no such thing as coincidence. Things happen for a reason. Those reasons may be man-made or divine. I thank God that he gave me the ability to put my brain back to work in new ways I never could before.

I have a special debt of gratitude to Paul Kengor. His wise counsel and sincere interest in my research gave me great motivation to move forward with this project.

He offered a realistic assessment of how my work might be received by traditional publishers as well as the criticism I can expect upon publication. He offered a needed critique on my initial preface and how to best present my theory to gain the utmost consideration.

Paul is a true titan in the conservative world. I thank him for his leadership and great scholarship.

Finally, I have the good fortune of a wonderful immediate family. My loving and dedicated wife of almost fifty years, a daughter who's a gifted writer, and a grandson with incredible creative talents are the absolute joys of my life. They give me reasons for living and motivation to take on challenging projects like this one. My love for them knows no measure.

J. C. Hawkins
St. Augustine, Florida

BIBLIOGRAPHY

This bibliography represents a partial compilation of the materials used to create the main thesis behind *Betrayal at Bethesda*. I highly recommend readers review these references and see how I gleaned factual material to synthesize my theory regarding the intertwined fates of James Forrestal, Joe McCarthy, and Jack Kennedy.

Ambrose, Stephen E. *Eisenhower, Volume One*. New York: Touchstone Books, 1983.

Anderson, Jack, with Daryl Gibson. *Peace, War and Politics: An Eyewitness Account*, New York, Tim Doherty Associates, 1997.

Baker, Russ. *Family of Secrets: The Bush Dynasty, America's Invisible Government, and the Hidden History of the Last Fifty Years*, New York, Bloomsbury Press, 2009.

Barron, John. *Operation Solo: The FBI's Man in the Kremlin*, Washington, DC, Regnery Publishing, 1995.

Belzer, Richard, and David Wayne. *Hit List*, New York, Skyhorse Publishing, 2013.

Black, Conrad. *Richard M. Nixon: A Life in Full*, New York, Public Affairs, 2007.

Blaine, Gerald with Lisa McCubbin. *The Kennedy Detail: JFK's Secret Service Agents Break Their Silence*, New York, Gallery Books, 2010.

Blair, Clay, Jr. and Joan Blair. *The Search for JFK*, New York, Berkley/ Putnam, 1976.

Brands, H.W. *The General vs. the President: MacArthur and Truman at the Brink of Nuclear War*, New York, Doubleday, 2016.

Chambers, G. Paul. *Head Shot: The Science behind the JFK Assassination*, expanded edition. Amherst, New York, Prometheus Books, 2012.

Corsi, Jerome R. *Who Really Killed Kennedy? 50 Years Later*, Washington, DC, WND Books, 2013.

DiEugenio, James. *Destiny Betrayed: JFK, Cuba and the Garrison Case*, New York, Sheridan Square Press, 1992.

Douglass, James W. *JFK and the Unspeakable: Why He Died and Why It Matters*, New York, Touchstone, 2008.

Doyle, William. *PT 109: An American Epic of War, Survival, and the Destiny of John F. Kennedy*, New York, William Morrow, 2015.

Eddowes, Michael H.B. *Khrushchev Killed Kennedy*, Dallas, Michael H. B. Eddowes self-published, 1975.

Evans, Medford. *The Assassination of Joe McCarthy*, Belmont, Massachusetts, Western Islands, 1970.

Evans, M. Stanton. *Blacklisted by History: The Untold Story of Senator Joe McCarthy and His Fight against America's Enemies*, New York, Crown Forum, 2007.

Evans, M. Stanton and Romerstein, Herbert. *Stalin's Secret Agents: The Subversion of Roosevelt's Government*, New York, Threshold Editions, 2012.

Farrell, John A. *Richard Nixon: The Life*, New York, Doubleday, 2017.

Frank, Jeffrey. *Ike and Dick: Portrait of a Strange Political Marriage*, New York, Simon & Schuster, 2013.

Garrison, Jim. *On the Trail of the Assassins*, New York, Skyhorse Publishing edition, 2012.

Gillon, Steven M. *The Kennedy Assassination, 24 Hours After: Lyndon B. Johnson's Pivotal First Day as President*, New York, Basic Books, 2009.

Groden, Robert J. *The Search for Lee Harvey Oswald*, New York, Penguin Studio Books, 1995.

Hamilton, Nigel. *JFK: Reckless Youth*, New York, Random House, 1992.

Herman, Arthur L. *Joseph McCarthy: Reexamining the Life and Legacy of America's Most Hated Senator*, New York, Free Press, 1999.

Herman, Arthur L. *Douglas MacArthur: American Warrior*, New York, Random House, 2016.

Janney, Peter. *Mary's Mosaic: The CIA Conspiracy to Murder John F. Kennedy, Mary Pinchot Meyer, and Their Vision for World Peace*, New York, Skyhorse Publishing, 2012.

Kengor, Paul. *Dupes: How America's Adversaries Have Manipulated Progressives for a Century*, ISI Books, Wilmington, Delaware, 2010.

Kengor, Paul. *The Communist, Frank Marshall Davis: The Untold Story of Barack Obama's Mentor*, New York, Threshold Editions, Mercury Ink, 2012.

Klara, Robert. *FDR's Funeral Train: A Betrayed Widow, a Soviet Spy, and a Presidency in the Balance*, New York, Palgrave Macmillan, 2010.

Koster, John. *Operation Snow: How a Soviet Mole in FDR's White House Triggered Pearl Harbor*, New York, MJF Books, 2012.

Kurtz, Michael L. *The JFK Assassination Debates: Lone Gunman versus Conspiracy*, Lawrence, KS, University Press of Kansas, 2006.

Lifton, David S. *Best Evidence: Disguise and Deception in the Assassination of John F. Kennedy*, New York, Macmillan Publishing Co., 1980.

Marrs, Jim. *Crossfire: The Plot That Killed Kennedy*, New York, Basic Books, 1989.

Mellen, Joan. *A Farewell to Justice*: *Jim Garrison, JFK's Assassination, and the Case That Should Have Changed History*, Dulles, Virginia, Potomac Books, 2005.

Morgan, Ted. *Reds: McCarthyism in Twentieth-Century America*, New York, Random House, 2003.

Nasaw, David. *The Patriarch: The Remarkable Life and Turbulent Times of Joseph P. Kennedy*, New York, The Penguin Press, 2012.

Nash, George H. *Freedom Betrayed: Herbert Hoover's Secret History of the Second World War and Its Aftermath*, Stanford, California, Hoover Institution Press, 2011.

Neal, Steve. *Harry & Ike: The Partnership That Remade the Postwar World*, New York, A Lisa Drew Book, Scribner, 2001.

Nelson, Phillip F. *LBJ: The Mastermind of the JFK Assassination*, New York, Skyhorse Publishing, 2011.

Newman, John. *Oswald and the CIA: The Documented Truth about the Unknown Relationship between the US Government and the Alleged Killer of JFK*, New York, Skyhorse Publishing, 2008 edition.

Nichols, David A. *Ike and McCarthy: Dwight Eisenhower's Secret Campaign against Joseph McCarthy*, New York, Simon & Schuster, 2017.

Nolan, Patrick. *CIA Rogues and the Killing of the Kennedys*, New York, Skyhorse Publishing, 2013.

Pacepa, Ion Mihai, and Ronald J. Rychlak. *Disinformation*, Washington, DC, WND Books, 2013.

Pepper, William E. *Orders to Kill: The Truth behind the Murder of Martin Luther King,* New York, Carroll & Graf Publishers, 1995.

Prouty, L. Fletcher. *JFK: The CIA, Vietnam and the Plot to Assassinate John F. Kennedy*, New York, Skyhorse Publishing, Barnes & Noble edition, 2013.

Ray, John Larry, and Lyndon Barsten. *Truth at Last: The Untold Story behind James Earl Ray and the Assassination of Martin Luther King, Jr.*, Guilford, Connecticut, The Lyons Press, 2008.

Reeves, Thomas C. *A Question of Character: A Life of John F. Kennedy*, New York, The Free Press, 1991.

Romerstein, Herbert, and Eric Breindel. *The Venona Secrets: Exposing Soviet Espionage and America's Traitors*, Washington, DC, Regnery Publishing, 2000.

Russell, Dick. *On the Trail of the JFK Assassins: A Groundbreaking Look at America's Most Infamous Conspiracy*, New York, Skyhorse Publishing, 2008.

Sale, Richard. *Traitors*, New York, Berkeley Publishing Group, 2003.

Shenon, Philip. *A Cruel and Shocking Act: The Secret History of the Kennedy Assassination*, New York, Henry Holt, 2013.

Smith, Amanda, ed. *Hostage to Fortune: The Letters of Joseph P. Kennedy*, New York, Viking Penguin, 2001.

Stinnett, Robert B. *Day of Deceit: The Truth about FDR and Pearl Harbor*, New York, Touchstone, 2001.

Stone, Roger, with Mike Colapietro. *The Man Who Killed Kennedy: The Case against LBJ*, New York, Skyhorse Publishing, 2013.

Stormer, John A. *None Dare Call It Treason…25 Years Later,* Florissant, Missouri, Liberty Bell Press, 1992.

Talbot, David. *Brothers: The Hidden History of the Kennedy Years*, New York, Free Press, 2007.

Talbot, David. *The Devil's Chessboard: Allen Dulles, the CIA and the Rise of America's Secret Government*, New York, HarperCollins Publishers, 2015.

Timmerman, Kenneth R. *Shadow Warriors: The Untold Story of Traitors, Saboteurs, and the Party of Surrender*, New York, Crown Forum, 2007.

Trento, Joseph J. *The Secret History of the CIA*, New York, MJF Books, 2001.

Tye, Larry. *Bobby Kennedy: The Making of a Liberal Icon*, New York, Random House, 2016.

Waldron, Lamar, with Thom Hartmann. *Legacy of Secrecy: The Long Shadow of the JFK Assassination*, Berkeley, California, Counterpoint, 2009.

Waller, Douglas. *Wild Bill Donovan: The Spymaster Who Created the OSS and Modern American Espionage*, New York, Free Press, 2011.

Weiner, Tim. *Legacy of Ashes: The History of the CIA*, New York, Anchor Books edition, 2008.

Weiner, Tim. *Enemies: A History of the FBI*, New York, Random House Trade Paperbacks, 2012.

Welch, Robert. *The Politician*, Belmont, Massachusetts, Belmont Publishing, 1963.

West, Diana. *American Betrayal: The Secret Assault on Our Nation's Character*, New York, St. Martin's Press, 2013.

Widmer, Ted. *Listening In: The Secret White House Recordings of John F. Kennedy*, New York, Hyperion, 2012.

Wilcox, Robert. *Target Patton: The Plot to Assassinate General George S. Patton*, Washington, DC, Regnery Publishing, 2008.

Wilcox, Robert. *Target JFK: The Spy Who Killed Kennedy?* Washington, DC, Regnery History, 2016.

Wrone, David R. *The Zapruder Film: Reframing JFK's Assassination*, Lawrence, KS, University of Kansas Press, 2003.

Made in the USA
San Bernardino, CA
02 August 2020